Writing
Articles *from the*
Heart

Writing Articles *from the* Heart

How to write & sell your life experiences

Marjorie Holmes

WRITER'S DIGEST BOOKS
CINCINNATI, OHIO
www.writersdigest.com

About the Author

Marjorie Holmes has written the type of personal essays and inspirational articles she describes in *Writing Articles From the Heart* for *Ladies' Home Journal, Reader's Digest, McCall's, Family Circle* and *Woman's Day*. Many of her articles and columns have been compiled into books, including *Love and Laughter* and *Beauty in Your Own Backyard*. Her seven books of essays and conversational prayers, including *I've Got to Talk to Someone, God* and *To Help You Through the Hurting*, have sold more than five million copies. She lives in McMurray, Pennsylvania.

Writing Articles From the Heart. Copyright © 1993 by Marjorie Holmes. Printed and bound in the United States of America. All rights reserved. No part of this book may be reproduced in any form or by any electronic or mechanical means including information storage and retrieval systems without permission in writing from the publisher, except by a reviewer, who may quote brief passages in a review. Published by Writer's Digest Books, an imprint of F&W Publications, Inc., 1507 Dana Avenue, Cincinnati, Ohio 45207. First paperback edition 2000.

Other fine Writer's Digest Books are available from your local bookstore or direct from the publisher.

Visit our Web site at www.writersdigest.com for information on more resources for writers.

To receive a free weekly E-mail newsletter delivering tips and updates about writing and about Writer's Digest products, send an E-mail with the message "Subscribe Newsletter" to newsletter-request@writersdigest.com or register directly at our Web site at www.writersdigest.com.

04 03 02 01 00   5 4 3 2 1

Library of Congress has catalogued hard copy edition as follows:

Holmes, Marjorie.
    Writing articles from the heart: how to write & sell your life experiences / by Marjorie Holmes.—1st ed.
        p.   cm.
    A great part of the material is taken from: Writing the creative article. 1969.
    Includes index.
    ISBN 0-89879-540-0 (hard cover)
    1. Authorship.   I. Title.
PN147.H63   1993
808'.02—dc20
ISBN 0-89879-988-0 (pbk: alk. paper)   92-37090
                                                         CIP

Edited by Jack Heffron
Interior designed by Sandy Conopeotis
Cover designed and illustrated by Melissa Riley/Tin Box Studio

For the two people who had
the greatest influence on my writing career:
Dewey Deal,
my inspiration at
Buena Vista College,
Storm Lake, Iowa.
And Professor Clyde Tull (Toppy),
at Cornell College,
Mount Vernon, Iowa.

Section 1:
Types of Articles From the Heart

CHAPTER 1   ## Writing From the Heart   7

A brief overview of the types of articles that allow you to express your personal vision and experience, and a test to gauge if you're the person to try them.

CHAPTER 2   ## The Magic of Getting Ideas   12

Tips for training your mind to generate and to recognize the article ideas that exist all around you.

CHAPTER 3   ## Personal Experience   24

How to use your memories, emotions, convictions, experiences and unique personality to create articles that will touch the hearts of your readers.

CHAPTER 4   ## Marriage   31

Learn to enrich and enlighten your readers by giving a personal touch to articles on love and marriage.

CHAPTER 5   ## Parents and Children   37

Since this subject affects so many readers, markets for articles about it are everywhere. Here's how to succeed in those markets by using your own experiences, ideas and feelings.

CHAPTER 6   ## Nostalgia and Memoirs   45

A guide to using the past to touch readers today.

CHAPTER 7   ## Controversial Topics   51

Keys to venting your objections and enthusiasms in provocative articles that will stir interest on both sides of any issue.

CHAPTER 8   ## Advice and Self-Help   57

Helping readers overcome obstacles and improve the quality of their lives requires a minimum of research and a maximum of honesty, insight and sincerity.

CHAPTER 9   ## Humor   62

Advice on how to brighten your articles with a light touch that will delight readers and editors.

CHAPTER 10   ## Essays, Sketches and Columns   71

How to pour your heart into three forms that will sell.

Section 2:
Writing Well From the Heart

CHAPTER 11   **The Five Fundamentals**   **83**
Learn the basics for all good creative articles, from provocative ideas to stirring conclusions.

CHAPTER 12   **Tone, Focus and Pace**   **91**
How to handle three crucial elements of writing from the heart.

CHAPTER 13   **Three Surefire Ways to Organize What You Have to Say**   **102**
These simple organizational patterns apply to every type of article from the heart.

CHAPTER 14   **Six Ways to Make Your Articles Better**   **110**
Improve your work and reach more readers through contrast and comparison, color, characterization, timeliness, specifics and memory devices.

CHAPTER 15   **Two More: Good Titles and Quotes**   **121**
Learn to add the gourmet touches that make a good article better and help it sell.

CHAPTER 16   **Twelve Secrets of Style**   **132**
Techniques for developing a writing style that will bring your individual voice to everything you write.

CHAPTER 17   **Methods and Markets**   **146**
Advice on how and where to sell your articles from the heart with tips on dealing successfully with editors.

CHAPTER 18   **Making the Most of Your Talent**   **155**
Keys to making the most of your talent along the road to becoming a published, professional writer—and after.

Index   **165**

Introduction

I am a born writer.

As a child my happiest hours were spent at a little desk my Grandpa Griffith made for me — a wonderful thing, cozy and secret, with cubbyholes. There I often sat scribbling while other kids were playing. And oh, the excitement the day my father brought home an old Oliver typewriter he'd bought at a sale for five dollars. On it I pecked out my first poems and stories. I could hardly wait for high school, which promised the magic of touch typing. Once there, I won all the medals for speed, and almost a portable typewriter: a prize offered by Smith Corona for copying text for fifteen minutes at sixty words a minute *without an error*. After the whistle blew I wept — I had been typing eighty-two words a minute! But they found two mistakes. The Smith man himself, was stricken, and so was my teacher. All they could do was give me another medal.

Looking back, all this racing seems symbolic. I think I was just in a hurry to get a job, work my way through college, and get on with the business of becoming a writer.

In college two professors provided guiding lights toward that goal: The first, a woman named Dewey Deal who had been my English teacher in junior high then by a remarkable stroke of fortune, for Freshman English at Buena Vista, our small but excellent hometown college. Her first assignment: simply to write in our notebooks every day. Descriptions, dialogue, philosophy, no matter what, so long as it came from our own lives. "From the heart."

When our notebooks came back, the words she had written on mine were to profoundly affect my life:

"Marjorie, Marjorie, you *must* make the most of your talent. I can feel joy with these paragraphs, I can feel sorrow, I am moved by their imagery.

I know that if you want to badly enough you can write beautiful things for people who crave beautiful things. There is a *duty!*"

The second powerful influence was Toppy Tull at Cornell College, a somewhat larger Iowa school, where I transferred after two years, mainly because he had a reputation of helping young writers get started. His wife, Jewell Bothwell Tull, was a popular selling author; both of them taught the classes, and published a campus magazine, *The Husk*, which not only gave students exposure, but often had contributions from giants like their friend Carl Sandburg.

Toppy's assignments were direct and practical: Quoting Samuel Johnson, "No man but a blockhead ever wrote except for money," he made us send our stuff out — to paying markets however small, where there was some chance of acceptance.

To my own amazement, I began to sell. To minor magazines, yes, the checks minuscule. But manna from heaven in those Depression days. And even more important, Toppy's pronouncement at that first check: "Now you are a pro. Go out there and *write!*"

But the most valuable advice he gave us was to study our writers' magazines. "They will teach you everything you need to know."

Thanks to Toppy Tull, Samuel Johnson, and those magazines, I did become a professional. Writing was the one thing I knew I had to do, and my goal was to sell — I needed the money. But it was Dewey Deal's words about talent and duty that had the greater impact on my writing itself. She made me realize the joy, and even the responsibility, of self-expression. Sharing your own pains and delights and marvelings with other people. In other words, *writing from the heart.*

After graduating, I married, and had a fling in radio — mainly to get it out of my system. But one day I realized, "This is *not* what I really want to do," and gave notice, packed up, and walked out forever on other people's places of business. I would have my own desk again — with or without cubbyholes. My own typewriter — even if, heaven forbid, that dear old Oliver! I would stay home and be a full-time writer. (If you don't count raising a family.)

And despite many rejections, it worked. Mainly because I discovered creative articles. Self-help, human interest, art of living pieces that require little or no research, because they are written out of your own mind and heart. While I did sell a lot of short stories, and eventually the novel on which I was laboring, fiction took longer and was much harder to place. But this form of writing never failed. I needed only to stop, and write a short, bright article, based on my own ideas and experiences, to enjoy that marvelous restorative — an acceptance. The check might be small, or sometimes impressive, but invariably it came, although not always on the first submission. For me it was the quickest road to paid publication. But even better, it said what I wanted to say. And there is no greater satisfaction, no matter who you are, if you have stories in your heart you long to share.

I figured out how to do it, and even wrote a book about it, focusing mainly on techniques and markets for the aspiring writer. *Writing Articles From the Heart* contains some of the same information. It is still addressed to everyone who has the talent, desire and discipline to become a successful writer.

And it still reaches out to everyone who *could* write, and meant to write, but whose first bright promise was never fulfilled. How often this dream is supplanted by other work, or suppressed, devoured by life's demands, or postponed until you can "find time for it." Or maybe you're one of the many who started out to be a writer but never finished. Often very talented people just don't have the fierce determination, confidence and patience to cope with rejections. They get discouraged and quit too soon. In others, the talent may have lain dormant and undiscovered until late in life. (Sometimes, though rarely, such a late blooming writer bursts onto the scene with a best-seller.)

But whatever your category, this book will bestir you and help you. It might even help you make up for lost time and get you started again.

Not all people are writers.

The book you hold in your hand also reaches out to another, even larger, audience. True, "There's a novel in every life story," as has been said; unfortunately, not everybody can write a novel. But everybody has ideas, convictions, and often personal stories that beg to be written. I believe that everybody should try to write them, if only for the sheer joy of self-expression: memories, adventures, experiences in love and marriage, raising children, sickness and health — the list is endless. And there is in most of us a desire to speak out, to be heard, to share our discoveries with other people.

You may be doing this already, in letters to newspapers and magazines, as well as to relatives and friends — and sometimes to people like me. If so, the creative article, written from the heart, might be another outlet for you. This book will show you how the professionals do it. It can even help you write better.

Or you may be working on your memoirs. If so, great! Go to it. I encourage everybody to write his or her own life story. It's actually important history. Some universities even collect memoirs. But I also advise the many people who ask me: "Write mainly for the joy of reliving it. Get it down on paper. That way you'll never lose it, and it will be a priceless legacy to your family."

Writing Articles From the Heart can help anyone who longs to write, for whatever reason. Read it, I repeat, to see how successful writers do it. The rules and secrets are here: How to recognize good ideas. How to organize your material to make it more effective. How to improve your style so that people will enjoy reading whatever you produce. Above all, how to reach the hearts of others who have the same pains and problems, who can be helped and inspired by what you have to say.

As that first teacher told me so long ago — the world is so hungry for answers. For a moment of beauty, a voice, a sentence, a song that will make their own hearts sing.

If, perhaps, that voice is yours, remember:
There is a duty!

Section 1
Types of Articles From the Heart

CHAPTER ONE

Writing From the Heart

*a*rticles from the heart are neither fact nor fiction, although they contain elements of both. They must be creative. They deal with human relationships. They are articles in which ideas are more important than facts, and whose purpose is to help, teach, amuse, move or inspire. Preferably doing all these things at the same time. Above all, they must be sincere — in short, written from the heart.

A large order? Not if you are equipped to write them. And the advantages are many. As I've said, such creative articles require almost no legwork — you seldom need to leave the house. They are less complicated to write than fiction, and since so few magazines use short stories anymore, easier to sell. You don't need an agent. And although some editors are prejudiced against "think pieces" except from the experts, really good ones are welcome in most newspapers and magazines, often are featured on the covers, and snapped up for reprints.

This brings us to the question, "Why creative?" True, all good writing demands creative ability, whether it be a report on superhighways, supermarkets or supermen. And the best fact articles shine with the creative personality that has deftly marshaled and meshed the facts. But the truly creative article, like fiction, emerges entirely out of the author's own vision and experience of life. And while you may (and should) support it with the testimony of others to provide some proof of what you say, the originality of your own concept and conviction dominates. You are writing from the heart.

Are you the person to try them?

If so, you've probably had at least a mild flirtation with fiction. You have an ear for dialogue, are fascinated by character — what makes people tick. You can dramatize, or learn to. Good articles read like stories, peppered with anecdotes or little scenes. A favored technique is the anecdotal opening, wherein the reader is hooked and lured into your subject. Some writers carry this so far it's hard for a reader to tell for a few paragraphs whether he's reading an article or a story. This I don't recommend, but the creative article writer should have imagination and the ability to compress action into a telling illustration.

Next, you probably like to give advice. People confide their troubles to you. And though your solutions might not always *work*, they sound great. You probably react first with emotion, then with logic, not only to their problems but your own. (The creative article needs both.)

You must basically be an optimist, in love with life, and whatever blows it deals you, you're just busting out all over with schemes for making it better: How to get along with the neighbors, your husband or yourself; how to find beauty in the ordinary, to deal with dread, to come through hell—if not unblistered, at least without third-degree burns. Articles from the heart must be life-affirming, hopeful, positive.

Fundamentally, you have to be an egotist whose ideas and experiences seem so vital you simply must express them, if not in fiction, then in its first cousin—essays and articles which will convey your enthusiasms, your ideals and fervent beliefs.

Finally, you should have, or be able to develop, a sense of organization and a smooth, friendly, but never didactic style. If you can add a twist of wit, a dash of humor, so much the better. Quite apart from the value and freshness of the original ideas, *it is the way they are written* that makes such articles sell.

Categories

The creative article can be any of the following:

1. Advice
2. Personal experience
3. Protest and controversy
4. Essays and sketches
5. Nostalgia
6. Humor
7. Inspiration

Obviously the categories overlap. For instance, it would be impossible to give advice without bringing in personal experience, perhaps nostalgia, maybe even controversy — and let's hope the advice is inspiring. The same is true for others. But there are definite differences among article types.

1. The *Advice* article is exactly that. It deals with the just mentioned how-to's. A classic example that may have started the whole trend is Dale Carnegie's famous book, *How to Win Friends and Influence People*. Articles of this genre often use the words "how to," actual or implied, in the title. Here are some of mine: "How to Make Home Life Happy," "Keep Your Husband in Your Arms." Or they use do's and don'ts in the same fashion: "Get Rid of That Gun," "Don't Be Afraid to be Friendly."

If the idea hasn't been done to death, and if the advice is entertaining as well as valid, it will always have a large audience of readers.

2. The *Personal Experience* article doesn't attempt to advise but rather to tell some dramatic or significant story from your own life or of someone in your family. A true adventure or experience. Something so interesting that others will want to hear about it but also often conveying truths worth remembering. Almost every family is rich in such stories: The time "Grandpa Was Chased by the Wolves," "The Day Dad Lost His Job and the House Burned Down," "Why We Bought the Elephant." And every individual has his own adventures and memorable experiences that beg to be told.

Reader's Digest calls such stories "Drama in Real Life." They buy good ones, and pay handsomely for them. *Guideposts* publishes no other kind. Study these magazines to absorb their special form and feeling. They offer perfect examples of articles from the heart.

The span of human experience is wide. It embraces birth and death, sickness and health, joy and pain. It knows no age barriers, and its adventures as well as its problems are shared by both men and women. You can write about *anything that happens to you* — if you write well enough to make it interesting and even helpful to other people.

3. In the *Protest and Controversy* article, you simply sound off, with fire, fervor and some good strong logic, about whatever bugs you. In short, you are attacking something you deplore: "Down With Junk Mail," "I'm Sick of All This Sex," "How Dare They Send Women to War?"

Or, conversely, you go to bat defending something others may deplore: "A Mother Speaks Up for Censorship," "Men *Are* Smarter Than Women — Thank Goodness!", "In Praise of Christmas Letters." If you make some people angry, so much the better; they will read it only to disagree. You'll be surprised, though, how many come out cheering.

4. *Essays and Sketches* are hard to define. Their purpose is not to advise or protest, but to observe, to express something moving, significant or lovely about the things we usually take for granted. Seldom as long as an article, perhaps a little longer than a column, they are simply sketches; if artfully done, prose poems. You will find them blooming like unexpected flowers in newspapers and a wide variety of magazines.

The first one I discovered was in *Better Homes and Gardens* while waiting for the dentist one day. It inspired me to rush home and write "The Swing," about the magic and wonder of a backyard swing. *Better Homes* not only loved it, they asked for more. This led to longer, deeper articles from the heart. And thus was launched one of the happiest relationships of my career. (Moral: It pays to read the magazines.)

5. For *Nostalgia*, you need mostly a vivid memory and a colorful style. You don't actually have to believe that the good old days were better, but you write about them with fondness and good humor.

My trips down memory lane started with magazine articles. I did an entire series for *Today's Health*, using such titles as: "Golden Days in Grandpa's Garden," "Washday at Dawn, Clothes on the Line," "The Days of Movie Magic," "Whatever Happened to Run Sheep, Run?", "A Lizzie, My Love, and You." All were very popular, both there and those that appeared in *Reader's Digest*. Later I gathered them into a book titled *You and I and Yesterday*, which became a best-seller for William Morrow. To our surprise, it made a tremendous hit with young people.

Harvesting your memories like this is great fun, whether you ever publish them or not. But if well done, readers of all ages will enjoy them.

6. *Humor* is forever popular, and editors are mad for it. But to be born with a literary funny bone is about as rare a gift as ESP. Nevertheless, born humorists do exist; every generation produces a bright new crop. The famous ones write syndicated columns as well as articles and best-

selling books. You'll often find others just as funny, I think, in your own newspapers. Read them, not only to laugh, but to learn.

And even if you don't intend to specialize in the humorous article, a touch of humor will brighten and add to the charm of whatever else you attempt.

7. The *Inspirational* article is a cross between the essay, advice and personal experience piece. It sticks to a single theme, and that theme is also always something positive, constructive and good. A symbol is frequently used to enhance or point up the theme.

For example, in one of *Guideposts'* articles, "The Afterglow," I used the lingering band of color after a sunset that my mother believed meant hope. *Don't worry, be patient, we can make it — things will get better soon.*

The inspirational article is by its very nature inescapably from the heart. In it the writer discusses and illustrates some discovery he has made about the art of living, with the goal of moving others to do likewise. He may even gently offer a few suggestions. But he never preaches or dictates, he simply — well, *inspires.*

To me it's heartening that so many warm, upbeat creative articles are being published. It proves than an awful lot of readers are weary of crime, violence, sex, disease and trouble. People still long for hope, tenderness, encouragement, humor, and some path to inner peace.

If you can offer these qualities in your writing, you will be helping many others, and at the same time enjoying the rewards of seeing your work in print. As I said, such articles don't take much time; they require little or no research; you can write them wherever you are.

Some editors call them "top of the head." But to me they will always be *deep of the heart.*

CHAPTER TWO

The Magic of Getting Ideas

here do you get your ideas?

That question is probably asked of writers more often than any other.

Ideas, by their very nature, have a kind of magic — as if springing from some mysterious source. For there is a certain magic about all creative writing, just as there is about any art. The writer or artist must first possess that magic lamp — talent — capable of producing the genie of ideas. The genie may come unbidden, but more often he appears with his rich treasure because the possessor of the lamp (the writer or artist) has learned how to summon him.

Thus, to that original question the experienced writer can only reply, "Where do you *stop* getting ideas?" Having trained himself to be aware, and to recognize ideas, his problem is far less one of lack than of selection. Almost literally there is no person, situation, emotion or experience, no remark, whether witty or mundane, even no object however humble that couldn't generate for him an idea, or a dozen, for a creative article.

Once a writer has achieved this happy state, he may find it hard to remember that the simple business of finding something to write about is often a problem for the beginner. Yet, if he's honest, he will recall a time when he too felt the awful burning of his special lamp, yet seemed powerless to release the genie who would produce ideas. How, then, did he free the genie? *By sitting down and writing.*

Don't Wait, Write

The first step any writer takes toward the "magic" that seems to come with professionalism is simply to sit down and write. The idea that launches you may be good, bad or indifferent; but the only way to move on toward other, perhaps better, ideas is to get rid of the one you have.

For many people this is extremely difficult. They procrastinate for fear that, having used up that one precious idea, there will be nothing else to take its place. Everywhere I go I meet someone who has "an idea" for an article or story. Often he's had it for years. He asks about how to handle it; he wonders if he should copyright it in case an editor tries to steal it. Very often he begs the professional writer to write it for him (for half the proceeds) to spare himself the ordeal of coping with it alone, and thereafter becoming bereft of ideas.

Such one-idea specialists never become writers. They don't even qualify for kindergarten in the long, hard school of writing—which requires them to establish regular working habits. Perhaps this is just as well, for they are motivated more by the persistent wish to be published than by the burning need to write.

The truly creative person (and the only one who should tackle either fiction or the creative article) *must* write, whether or not he seems to have anything to write about. He is drawn to his desk almost against his will. He may think of excuses to postpone the misery of perhaps finding he has no ideas, but in the end he submits, and begins to discipline himself to a daily stint.

Once this happens, a remarkable thing occurs: Ideas come. And ideas were not meant to be hoarded. Like the cow that must be milked, or the flowers that must be picked to continue blooming, ideas must be spent. And the more prodigal you are with your thoughts, the more enriched your imagination and creative skills become. In the throes of one article or story, you often find so many new ideas popping up clamoring for attention that you can hardly wait to finish what you're doing and get on with the next.

Recognizing Ideas

Too many would-be writers grope blindly for ideas, unable to recognize the wonderful treasury waiting in their own life stories.

After my first lecture in the course I taught at Georgetown University in Washington, D.C., a student sent me a note in desperation. She had a consuming longing to write, and a brisk, deft style — but, she claimed, "I don't know what to write about. I am absolutely devoid of ideas."

One day, having coffee with her after class, I discovered that she was English, had a radiant personality and a bubbling fund of hilarious anecdotes from her travels all over the world. Her husband was in the diplomatic corps. She deplored the constant rounds of entertaining, the constant uprooting of herself and their children. As she spoke, I kept interrupting with, "There's an idea": the false faces people wear to cocktail parties; how to inure yourself to such affairs when you don't feel like going; the wild and wonderful comparisons between British and American schools; how to get along with a husband whose career is travel when you long only to settle down with a pot of tea and a good book.

Her heart was spilling over, and mine responded: Nothing to write about? She was loaded! She had simply never taken a warm, positive, professional look at herself. Failing to recognize the wealth of material in her own experience, she had spent none of it; hence her imagination failed to function constructively. She had not found any *angle of interpretation*, which is actually the crux of the creative article idea. I discuss angle of interpretation at greater length in chapter 12.

On the other hand, there are people who have traveled extensively and perhaps lived abundantly who are eager to write about it because they have "all this marvelous material." And they are certainly to be encouraged. We need and want such stories. But it is not enough simply to relate your observations or experiences, no matter how deeply felt. You, the author, must point and shape them to some fresh lesson or purpose. In essence, find that cogent *angle of interpretation*.

To recognize good ideas you must be constantly alert to the possibilities in your own heart and head. Remember, *you are your own best source*. Keep diaries and journals, *expecting* usable ideas to pop out of them. The very anticipation works a kind of magic. And when a good idea hits you, what a thrill! Every true writer feels it. Also, read, read, read — the more creative articles the better. Other people's ideas will help you rub your magic lamp and summon your own bountiful genie of ideas.

Learning to Train Your Mind

That marvelous instrument, the mind, has for all practical, useful purposes, two layers: the conscious and the unconscious. The writer learns to use both in the begetting of ideas.

Let's consider first the unconscious, that layer of mind that suddenly awakens, brimming with thoughts when the rest of you wants to sleep. If you're worried, it thrashes about incessantly, seeking solutions. If you've had a stimulating experience, the unconscious keeps replaying it. In short, its activity is always triggered by a thought, event, experience, person. Thus, if you really want a good idea, or some fortifying ones for the piece you're working on, try this: Simply read several good articles in similar vein before settling down. Or merely read a number of titles! Then close your eyes and relax while the ideas come zooming in.

It's a very old trick that I learned from a college art teacher who advised us to look at books of design or paintings before going to bed: "You'll be surprised at how many new, underivative yet excellent pictures will leap from your unconscious." This was true; it worked, and has been working for me ever since. Other writers verify this; some even keep couches in their studies for this purpose. (I used to, but mine always got so covered up with papers I could never find it.)

The first creative article I ever wrote was the result of my reading through a single issue of a magazine giving guidelines for better living, written in a friendly, informal and engaging style. When I put down that magazine and turned out the lights, my mind presented me with a whole flock of thoughts. One of them was so insistent that I got up and began to write. Before morning I had finished a 1,500-word piece, "You Can Be Too Good a Sport," which was promptly bought. This is also a demonstration of that well-known law: *Write the kind of thing you read*. The advice is good for more than one reason. If you read the magazines you want to write for, you are learning to slant toward a definite market. And meanwhile, your unconscious is absorbing a certain tone and rhythm of writing, and storing up that curious power that in turn creates your own ideas.

Once you have established the writing habit, the clamor of creative ideas will not be limited to the time you spend at the typewriter. Your unconscious will present them to you while you are doing things totally unrelated to writing — shingling the roof, riding on a subway, scrubbing the floor. Much as I deplore time-consuming housework, it is sometimes an advantage to have to clean up the kitchen or vacuum before getting to my study. The mind has to occupy itself with something, and more often than not, it ponders the complexities of personal relationships, situations with family or neighbors, scraps of dialogue, little scenes that reveal human nature, memories. All the teeming stuff of the creative article. And out of it will suddenly come winging a phrase, a slant, frequently a title that itself proposes or states the premise of a likely piece. Whatever you are occupied with, if you write regularly, your unconscious will keep you tuned and focused toward more writing, productive writing, by constantly feeding you ideas. It will become your best ally.

There are also methods you can consciously apply and definite places you can look for ideas. Let's consider just one. Train your mind *consciously* to get to work on your next writing project even as you ride that subway, shingle that roof or scrub that floor. Direct it toward the basic idea, and let it start sorting and assembling the peripheral ideas that will appear. This kind of mental discipline is invaluable. It will spare you the frustration that comes with delays and save you time. You will find that a great deal has been accomplished by the time you reach your desk.

Where the Ideas Are

Yourself

Obviously, as I've said, you yourself are the best source of ideas for articles from the heart: your reaction to the human condition, and suggestions for improving it (advice); your righteous indignation (protest); your spiritual growth (inspiration); your adventures, simple or dramatic (personal experience); your memories (nostalgia, or the reflective sketch); the things that make you laugh (humor).

This does not mean that the pronoun "I" will pepper your articles; it must be used judiciously. But since yours is the viewpoint and yours the voice, you the writer are the most vital source of material you can have.

But suppose ideas don't simply come raining down as a reward for your diligent labors, your mental alertness, and your fervent belief in yourself. Are there places where you can look for more ideas? Indeed there are:

Newspapers

People who write fact articles constantly scan the newspapers for stories of people, places and projects that they can *investigate* and expand. The writer of articles from the heart should read newspapers with his senses attuned to the emotions behind the story. Just as in fiction, he wonders — what motivates people? How do they *feel*?

Marching before us in newsprint we see the panorama of the human condition. Tragedy and comedy, failures and triumphs, weddings and divorces, graduations, births and deaths. From events as critical as murders and rapes and war, to the simplest tale of a boy and his dog — look deeper and you feel the pulse of life. The faces in the photos speak to you; the brides are usually beaming, other faces may be frightened, the eyes forlorn, angry or pleading. What are they trying to tell you? How could you help them? If you could have an honest heart-to-heart talk with them, what would you learn?

Reporters are trained to be objective, and interviews are not your job. But the creative writer searches, above all he identifies — their story becomes your story. This is an enriching process that will deepen your understanding and enable you to speak the language of life more clearly. Thus when you use your God-given talent to write, you will be fulfilling your purpose — to reach as many people as possible, and hopefully make life a little brighter.

So, you can see how even a page or two of your daily newspaper can spark excellent ideas.

Another more obvious source is the letters written to what were once more aptly called the Lovelorn columns. Now they're titled "*Ann Landers*," "*Dear Abby*" — or the name of some other wise and caring columnist. Here, as nowhere else, people pour out their troubles and beg for advice. Their stories run the gamut of human conflict. And they represent both release and trust. Like most people they've "got to talk to somebody,

God," in a way that doesn't risk betrayal; and the answers they get are usually just good, keen, comforting but often tough common sense. If the advice sometimes backfires and readers disagree, there is a flood of protest, which is itself enlightening to the creative article writer.

These columns are well worth reading, if only to ask yourself: What do I feel about this? What would *I* have told that brutalized wife? That pregnant teenager? That man who lost his job while his wife was promoted.

As a writer you too are involved. New and better ideas pop up, not only for this situation but others.

Conversations

For the same reason, tune in on other people's conversations, as well as your own. Listen to what people are saying at parties, at work, on subways and buses. Once, sitting behind a mother and her long-haired son, I heard him threaten, "Okay, if I can't get a motorcycle I'll get married." Wow! Where could you find a funnier, more flagrant line to launch an article on any of the following subjects: "The Me Generation," "The Scared-Parent Syndrome," "What's happened to marriage values?" (Matrimony versus motorbike.)

But not all such conversations are so flippant. I've personally had long, heartrending conversations with total strangers on public transportation. Once, a woman straight from the judge's chamber after her divorce. She was still mad. "Another woman. We have two kids and the louse won't even pay me a dime." I agreed this was terrible, and we both perked up and had a great ride just being mad at *men*. Another time, a poor guy en route to buy flowers for his little girl's casket. "Barely eight years old. Killed by a drunken driver." He showed me her picture. "Why, she's beautiful!" I could exclaim honestly. "Yeah." He wiped his eyes. "Looked just like her mother, an angel—I never could figure out what she saw in me." He told me all about it. A story of poverty and pain and love. By the time I got off, both of us were crying. And waving to that pathetic young face in the window, suddenly I couldn't stand it. I had to *do* something, say something, give him some money—but the doors were closing, the bus wouldn't stop even when I ran after it, pounding.

I was too late, even to get his address. All I could do now was comfort myself (and perhaps other people) by writing about it. An article or column about showing compassion—if possible, in time to help someone who really needs it.

Most people like to talk. Listen to them, wherever you go, whoever they are. Listen to your neighbors, to cabdrivers, hairdressers, repairmen, your baby-sitter, the woman who cleans your house. A writer never "wastes time" by having such conversations; instead he gains ideas and understanding. Each of us is extraordinary in our own way, whatever our job. With stories to be shared, straight from the heart. Draw other people out. Often their experiences are amazing, their philosophy profound. Some of the wisest utterances I ever heard came from the lips of an old hobo who landed on our doorstep one day when I was coping with my first baby and struggling to fix up a run-down house. He moved in to the shed, and stayed until the job was done—and just as important, my notebook was bursting with his wry and solemn wit.

Out of such "dialogues in everyday living," as I called them in my own newspaper column, have come countless articles and books.

But don't overlook the ideas that spill out of conversations with friends and other people very much like yourself. They are so revealing, not only of their attitudes, but your own! The saying, "How do I know what I think till I hear what I have to say?" is true. Get together with someone who sparks your mental fireworks, and you may be amazed at what brilliant ideas you spout—concepts that lie slumbering unsuspected until they are awakened by the presence of this other personality. The creative writer needs at least a few creative friends. They don't have to be writers themselves, but people who do have good minds and can be articulate. The value is twofold: A bright friend has bright ideas, which he is usually delighted for you to use. Even better, his brightness fans yours.

But again, none of this will be of benefit unless you *keep that notebook*. Hasten to the typewriter and recap the conversation as accurately as you can. You probably won't use it in toto when it comes to the actual article, but it is important to catch the essence of what was said, and then shape and sharpen it to your purpose. It will have given you what you need— the vital idea.

Your Family

Your children. Your marriage. Your relatives.

No writer who has children should ever lack for ideas. The problems of parenthood are legion and the ways to solve them limitless. Whether you treat the complexities of rearing children humorously or seriously, the number and variety of possibilities — from the time you hold your first baby in your arms until you comb the rice out of your hair after the last one's wedding, and even beyond — should keep you stocked with ideas.

Marriage is another subject so important to the creative article writer that techniques of dealing with it will be discussed later. If yours is the ideal union, you can write what's good about it, and how come. The slant will be refreshing. If, as is more likely, you've noticed a few flaws in your own or other couples' marriages, the defects will provide the meat of many an article, serious or humorous, depending upon the style you bring to it.

As for relatives! Here ideas grow as numerous as leaves on the family tree. Brothers, sisters, cousins and colorful aunts; parents and grandparents. Amusing or inspiring tales and truths drawn from members of your clan. Countless publications welcome articles based on memorable characters — an eccentric grandparent, aunt, cousin; the teacher (or relative) who influenced your life; the unobtrusive person in your town who took on a cause and effected an important change for the better. Pets, too, fall into this category, since their relationship with their owners is often very close and important — especially in the case of elderly people who live alone. Or the writer who works alone.

Your Own Articles

In the body of every article you write lurk the seeds of several more. Watch for them. These other article ideas lie in the material you may have to discard because it throws the basic argument out of focus or makes the article too long. Or you may find them by reversing the idea you have just written.

To illustrate: In writing an article on communication, "How to Talk to the Person You Married," for *Better Homes and Gardens*, I originally included a number of common listening faults. The list was deemed too negative, and cut by the editors. Hating to let anything go to waste and still feeling I had not exhausted the subject (also still hearing the common complaint, "He never tells me anything"), I expanded that list into another article, "Why Men Don't Talk to Their Wives." Then, as I thought of counterarguments (you have to see both sides of any question), I wrote "Why Women Can't Talk to Their Husbands." Both new pieces were also published in *Better Homes and Gardens* and reprinted in *Reader's Digest*.

On another topic — family finances — I veered off on a tangent about working wives, a subject that is certainly of increasing importance. Out of this I wrote an article, "Whose Money Is It When Women Work?" Variations on this theme can be found in almost every issue of every major magazine and many specialized ones. For example, "What's Behind Those Fights About Money?" (*McCall's*); "Don't Wait for What You Want" — denying yourself the better things in life until a man gives them to you can mean waiting a lifetime (*New Woman*); "Love on a Shoestring" (*Redbook*); "Money Fights: Don't Let Them Ruin Your Marriage (*Ladies' Home Journal*).

If you have a truly creative mind, you will always find more to be said on any subject than there is space for. Write fully, then glean and winnow until you have a tight, strong article that says only one thing and says it well. But save all those peripheral ideas; the best ones can be turned into articles that may outshine the one from which they sprang.

As I have indicated, one major reason the beginner is often stymied for ideas is that he doesn't know what to do with the ones he has! And usually the reason the writer does not know is that he hasn't organized his life around the business of writing. Herein lies the value of writers' magazines, courses, and classes and conferences with professionals, books on technique and marketing. Any and all sources of stimulus and information that will not only goad him into writing regularly but show him how to develop an idea into something salable, then direct him where and how to go about selling the finished product, are valuable.

Read everything you can about the business of writing, just as you must read the magazines you want to write for. Get the feel and flow of it into your unconscious as well. Above all, write! The more you write, the more fiercely will burn that special lamp of your talent, and the more eager its genie will be to serve you, springing up at every turn, snatching ideas from the air and offering them to you in exciting new forms. Or, should he slumber, you'll have so mastered the magic of the lamp that you can summon him up at will.

Keep a Notebook

Conscious or unconscious — wherever they come from, ideas aren't much use unless you write them down. In addition to the habit of writing regularly, the second most valuable habit any writer can have is *keeping a notebook*.

By this I mean any form in which you set down these ideas while they are fresh. It can be a notepad carried in your pocket; it can be a loose-leaf journal. It can even be any scrap of paper on which you scribble, providing you later transpose your notes into something legible in a notebook, card file or Manila folder.

After years of using the loose-leaf journal method, I have come around to the folder. In this way, every new idea that seems worthy of a separate article can be titled, if only tentatively, and alphabetically filed. Every time I get a bright thought that might be worked into the article, it too can be roughly caught and tucked into the same folder. There also can be assembled any supplementary material such as quotes, pertinent anecdotes, clipped articles or references which might be useful.

For the new writer, the major value in keeping a notebook is to get him into the habit of writing ideas down — not only for the value of an individual idea, but for the greater benefit of generating new ideas. Even though he may not use all of them, his awareness is intensified, like a person who never notices coins or stamps or first editions until he starts to collect them — then he suddenly sees them everywhere.

Furthermore, the ideas begin to have value in themselves. While the writer can't use all of them, and probably won't sell all the articles he produces, the larger his fund of initial ideas the better his chances are.

But ideas are ephemeral things, likely to disappear. Whenever or wherever one occurs to you — don't wait, stop whatever you're doing and write it down. Tomorrow morning, or even an hour from now may be too late. Even if you do have a recollection of what it was all about, the essence of it, fresh and cogent and neatly phrased, may be gone. Fill your notebook with ideas now!

CHAPTER THREE

Personal Experience

*I*f you are truly a creative writer you'll find it almost impossible to separate yourself from your material, whether you're writing fact or fiction. Your memories, emotions, convictions, experiences and unique personality will permeate whatever you write. It will even influence what you choose to write about. And this is great! It is the special gift that makes your work worth reading because it rings true to life. Readers can feel and think *with* you; and they particularly savor the strong personal stories drawn from your own life.

Any article from the heart is by its very nature personal. But there are some types that are definitely more personal than others: reflective essays and sketches, nostalgia, articles on sex and love and family life. And first and foremost, the article based on a memorable, dramatic or significant personal experience.

Magazines have always favored true first-person stories, and they are publishing more than ever before. Editors have long realized that the most valid truths, as well as the most interesting adventures, are those that come straight out of human lives. This form of the article from the heart is often your best bet. I strongly recommend it even for people who aren't striving to become professional writers. Almost everybody is harboring at least one great story in his heart that deserves to be told.

The story itself may be so unique and dramatic that it commands attention; or it may be a fairly common experience which *becomes* dramatic in the telling. In either case, it must be written so that the average person can relate to it himself. The secret of its success is in the telling.

By drama the last thing we mean is heaving bosoms and scalding tears; posturings, pantings, mad dashes for freedom; voices that beg, scream, whine, implore — or any of the paraphernalia of action or emotion that bespeaks *melodrama*. Drama is simply the ability to portray a believable character, and to let the reader share that character's experience in the most intensely interesting and beneficial way.

The Fictional Techniques

This generally means adopting the techniques used so often in fiction: suspense, threat, rising drama; the flashback; moment of truth, and sometimes denouement. (Although not necessarily all.)

One major difference between the fictional short story and the personal experience article is in characterization. You, the author, are the major character (or someone very close to you); hence you cannot or need not give much of a physical description. Never, heaven forbid, use the "My mirror told me I was beautiful," approach; nor, "I am a tall husky specimen with curly hair," although little graphic touches can sometimes be worked in — "It was a big load even for my six-foot, two-hundred-pound frame." When well done, these touches can help the reader visualize, and they may be necessary sometimes to clarify the action.

Generally speaking, there is seldom need to go deeply into motivation; and there is seldom time, and rarely much reason to flashback into a lot of biographical data to establish character. You are simply onstage, and character is implicit in the way you react to the situation, and resolve it.

Furthermore, the character is always subordinate to the experience. You are not Exhibit A, you are merely the vehicle for Exhibit A, the experience. This is in contrast to the fact article, wherein a prominent or interesting person is being portrayed. There, the author interviews his subject, gathers all possible information about him, and draws his portrait for the public. Or the subject talks about himself in a question-answer format, or an "as told to" article; or if he can actually write, he may produce his own self-revelations.

In the creative type of personal experience article, however, the character is genuinely moved or changed in some way by the experience. And his prospect of *change* (opinion altered, lesson learned, etc.) is usually evident from the beginning. There is also suspense from the beginning. A hint of threat, impending danger, or sometimes disappointment or trouble ahead, which builds as you proceed.

To illustrate: Here is the opening for "Belle," a story about the crisis my family faced after our Dalmatian was cruelly hurt in a boating accident. It was published in *Guideposts* with the subheading, "If a beloved pet is in trouble, is it wrong to ask the Good Shepherd to heal her?"

We all knew our dog was doomed. After three long months in the hospital and three operations she was getting no better. And it was all my fault. Nobody blamed me, yet I felt so guilty.

"If Belle's got to be put to sleep," I insisted that awful morning of our decision, "I'm the one who should give the order . . . After all, I was driving the boat that night we hit her."

The family was finally out of the house. I paced the floor, struggling for courage. Get it over with — it was either this or amputate her leg. Finally, still crying, I strode to the phone. "Dr. Moseller? We've decided the most merciful thing would be to — let Belle go."

"Yes. Okay. I think you're right."

But I felt like an executioner, the story continues. As if I had ordered the death of one of our children. And suddenly, trying to drink a cup of coffee, I couldn't stand it. I panicked and ran back to the phone.

This time the circuits were busy. I dialed again and again. Finally, the doctor's aide was saying, "I'll see if I can catch him." Then the doctor himself was on the line . . . "Stop, wait, don't do it!"

In the silence that followed, my heart almost failed. "You caught me just in time. Are you sure?"

"Yes, no! Yes, it's got to be done, but wait until tonight, please. At least we can come down and tell her goodbye."

A bit sheepishly, I called my husband. And that night as we drove the forty miles to the small Virginia town where we had our summer cabin, we reminisced about Belle.

Here flashback was the perfect tool to describe the polka-dotted dog who loved to swim, and what happened that tragic night:

She was always the first out of the car, streaking for the water like a jubilant child. The skiers learned to swoop around her eagerly chugging head. Then we got another boat, secondhand but bigger and more powerful. . . . The teenagers wanted to try it out; I said I'd drive. . . . Belle was already dashing past. We heard the usual splash as she dived in.

I didn't think about her; it was enough just to concentrate on the controls, to watch and listen for the signals from my husband and the two tensely waiting skiers. "Hit it!" . . .

I pulled back the lever, we shot through the water . . . then that body-shattering jolt. The awful thud. Those wild, agonized yelps.

More suspense followed: Our frantic calls to find a vet this late. The long, desperate drive to get there, delayed by a bumpy detour around an interminable parade. Even so, the parade kept crossing our path, and when we finally arrived, the doctor couldn't give us much hope. He'd try to make her comfortable; if she made it till morning he might be able to operate, but even then. . . . He shook his head; she was torn limb from limb.

Belle made it through the summer, while he put her mangled body back together. But one leg refused to heal . . . and now here we were at the veterinarian's office bearing a final bag of treats. We could hear her barking, as if she sensed our presence. They wheeled her out on a little cart—and her tail was wagging! Wildly, despite the cast and bandages, she greeted us in an ecstatic frenzy. And when she licked our hands we knew we couldn't put her away.

The doctor read the message in the tears that ran down our faces. "Look, if you're willing to nurse her, why not take her home until you're sure?"

Rejoicing, we lifted Belle into the car.

Now the true depth of the whole adventure begins to emerge. The children couldn't believe it—the dead restored! All four of them took turns feeding and lifting and helping her hobble about. But we knew we had only postponed the inevitable.

Then I thought of prayer. I would tell Belle's story in my newspaper column and ask my readers to pray for her.

The paper was scarcely on the street when the phone began to ring. Prayer circles, churches, animal shelters, individuals. Then came the avalanche of mail. Belle even got get-well cards from other dogs. Had she any idea of the floods of love she had released? We knew only that two weeks later the doctor was amazed. *The hip was healing.* By the third week he could lessen the bindings; the fourth he removed the cast.

"It's a miracle," he said. "She'll have some arthritis, but she'll be swimming again next summer. This dog is well!"

The article concludes:

Belle lived four more years, battle-scarred, a little gimpy, but still a joy. And as she would stand, hips in perfect alignment, gazing at the water, the realization came to me: If all of us would pray for each other with the selfless warmth with which people prayed for Belle, miracles could occur for us too, every day.

What Readers Really Want

I hadn't done as well on an earlier piece I thought sure editors would be begging for. A true fish story, telling how our son, thirteen years old, caught an 8-foot, 100-pound marlin. (Four times the size of the one his dad had caught the year before, and paid a bundle to have mounted.) They brought the monster home at midnight, bedded on ice in the station wagon. It was to lie in state the next day, long enough for picture-taking, and the neighbor kids to admire. Then it would be disposed of, my husband had decreed. It simply didn't make sense to spend all that money on another *dead fish.*

Mark, of course, was frantic to keep the trophy, and so was his little brother who'd been along. Desperate scenes followed, ending in an equally desperate compromise. *We would do it ourselves!* "You kids start clearing the Ping Pong table, while your mother runs down to the library to see if they have a taxidermy book."

I returned clutching two slim volumes, dealing mostly with reptiles, birds and beasts and no fish larger than a bass. Even so, we copied down the lengthy list of rare chemicals, and sent our oldest daughter to six drugstores to find them, only to discover on the next page: "For professionals only. Beginners should use household Borax." My husband multiplied how much it would take to build a mold for a bass; then set forth in quest of seven bags of sand and 200 pounds of plaster of paris. . . .

By now the odor of fish was potent; if we were going to save that marlin we'd have to work fast. . . .

Those taxidermists earn their money. Our project took almost a year of somewhat frantic togetherness, before at last husband and sons carried it triumphantly into the living room, and from the wall Mark's mighty marlin returned our astounded gaze.

The story had everything, I thought: drama, humor and even suspense, as fervent hopes contend with the fears of failure. I called it, "How to Stuff a Fish," and sent it out — as usual to the highest paying prospects. Only to have that dratted fish keep swimming back! Always with those flattering rejections that make you want to weep. "Near-miss but . . ."; "Very entertaining, but. . . ." Finally the truth came out: "Not enough people go deep-sea fishing. Our readers wouldn't identify with it."

Identification. Of course! Those editors were right. My material was a little *too* narrow. To save it I would have to revise, making less of the unusual undertaking, more of the people behind it. Mark's disappointment, his dad's concern. In other words, giving it more *heart*. So, after a few more tries, I rewrote, retaining the humor but focusing more on emotions, this time from a man's viewpoint.

After a brief opening anecdote, he says:

> I have always had this old-fashioned notion that sons are some-thing a father's supposed to go fishing with. Having practiced this theory on all adjacent rivers, lakes and streams, we had started on the ocean, some sixty miles away. Both boys had been along, in fact, when I caught my own first marlin the year before. It was a mere stripling as marlins go, but thinking never to catch another, I'd decided to blow the $300 the taxidermist charged.
>
> This did not prepare me for what I'd do should one of the *kids*

catch one. . . . Or the pride I'd feel when we came in, flag flying, weighed it, and my son's fish proved the record for the season.

"You gonna keep him?" the captain asked.

That did the trick. I caught my own fish the next time I cast. *The Elks Magazine* made it even more applicable to their audience by the subheading: "What would you do if your son caught an eight-foot marlin? Have it mounted? Or try this alternative that would be good for the boy as well as your bank account." The illustrations were warm and tender— of an average American family hopefully working with their fish. All of it blended perfectly with the last line in our story:

> "Maybe like me, you're so foolish or old-fashioned as to take your sons fishing. If so, you may discover, as I did, that the most valuable trophies aren't always those you pay for with a check."

This is what keeps the personal experience article from being a mere grade-school exercise of Show and Tell. "Look at me! Aren't we clever, aren't we wise?" You aren't writing just to describe something exciting or call attention to yourself. Yes, the story must capture the reader's interest and be told well—never just a recitation of events that read like a diary or a letter home. But in addition, it should convey emotions the reader himself can feel, and leave him with some truth or lesson, some bit of understanding gained—perhaps even of himself.

In essence, the story from your heart will touch your readers' hearts as well.

CHAPTER FOUR

Marriage

As we see, article types overlap. Certainly there is nothing more personal to write about than love and marriage. The relationship between men and women is the oldest and most fascinating subject since time began. I always tell new writers, "Get the words Man, Woman, Husband, Wife, Love, Marriage or Sex into your title if you can. They always attract attention."

In writing about marriage, however, the average person may feel hopelessly unqualified, compared to the doctors, psychologists and marriage counselors already in the field. Often such experts are columnists or regular contributors to the magazines. The way many freelance writers get around this is to team up with an authority and co-author the article. Or they take a topic and quote one expert or several at length. By adding a few anecdotes and case histories, it's possible to come up with an excellent piece.

But for me, this is not writing a creative article in the true sense; to be creative it must come from the heart. Writing sincerely about marriage is to convey *your* ideas on the subject. It is this fundamental slant or concept that gives your article focus, and lends conviction to your tone and style.

There is, in fact, something very appealing about a frank, curbstone opinion, presented without apology, provided, of course, it is presented *well*. When I was first feeling my way, I came across an article written in this vein which impressed me. I failed to save it and can't remember who wrote it or where it appeared, but I do remember the special charm of its innocent: "I am just a housewife. I have no advanced degrees, and I barely squeaked through college. But I have been married ten years and feel I know a little something about the business of getting along with *anyone* to whom you've committed your life."

I am paraphrasing roughly, but her words were brisk, well chosen, and her arguments persuasive. Other women could identify with her from the opening shot, and would listen to what she had to say. I don't know whether that writer ever produced another article, but I do know that the sheer vigor and candor of her approach impressed me and helped me to produce mine. It dawned on me that anyone who writes sufficiently well and has something to say is entitled to be heard.

How Marriage Articles Differ

Marriage articles differ from the general category of Personal Experience, in which the author tells his true story of some dramatic or memorable *event*. A marriage article, as such, focuses on *one aspect* of the *subject*, presenting your ideas about its joys and problems, which may influence or inspire somebody else. Thus it could also fall into the advice category.

Your illustrations aren't necessarily personal. You don't have to bare your soul and risk embarrassing your mate. You just write what you think about the subject, from any viewpoint you choose. The joys and problems of marriage are universal. Everybody goes through them. That you know what you're talking about is implicit in the way you write about them.

I found two ways to do this: Lighthearted observations about some common conflicts in marriage, including bits of advice. (The style and tone cheerful, and often funny without being flippant.) Or more serious (but never ponderous) discussions and illustrations, exploring more serious subjects in greater depth.

Early in my own marriage, I flew blithely into the subject, solving everything likewise in that vein. This is obvious from a sampling of my titles: "Rules for Migrating Brides" (we moved a lot), "Fun Without Funds" (we had no choice), "Baby the Brute" (care and feeding of husbands), "Do Men Want Clever Wives?" (not always), "Is Real Love Jealous?", "Don't Let That First Quarrel Lick You," "Let's Have Tantrums" (things were getting a little rockier by then). And many more. These brisk bright pieces of about 1,000 words quickly found homes in the self-help magazines like *Your Life*, *The Man*, *The Woman*, and others being published at the time. And a few were beginning to land in homemaking magazines like *House Beautiful* and *American Home*.

Geraldine Rhoads, editor of *The Woman*, once had bought so many she asked me to hold off submitting for a while. This dear lady moved on to an excellent larger magazine, *Today's Woman*, which used both fiction and nonfiction, and ultimately became editor of *Woman's Day*, each time accepting the work of her favorite writers whenever she could. So don't be afraid of starting small. Small publications can often be the best route toward your goal.

Getting Two Articles From One

As time passed and the deeper issues of marriage surfaced, my articles got longer (up to 2,500 words) and had more substance. Again revealed by a sampling of my titles: "Can Husbands and Wives Be Friends?" "What is Your Paycheck Doing to Your Marriage?" "The Real Intimacy in Marriage." "Do You Dare to be Honest In Marriage?" "Yes, We Do Marry Our In-Laws."

Major markets were almost guaranteed. *Better Homes and Gardens* became *my* second home. A few light pieces and sketches had opened the door. Now they welcomed these marriage articles, publishing three or four a year. Two of the first proved to be blockbusters, with unexpected complications.

I called the first one, "What Every Woman Wants" (affection, attention, romance). I contrasted the basic attitudes men and women have toward marriage, and simply discussed, without anecdotes, how disappointed and disillusioned women can be when romantic attentions stop.

The article opens and proceeds, in part, as follows:

> There is one luxury that any man, rich or poor, can give his wife. It costs him nothing, yet it is the one thing his wife wants more than anything under heaven. But, by some perverse force of fate, it is also the one thing the average male puts the least stock in.
>
> The American husband has many virtues. He works hard. He buys more insurance against illness, accident, old age and his own demise than any man in the world. He is usually loyal. When he says, "I won't be home for dinner, dear, I've got to work," most women can believe him.

He can be counted on not only because he's basically decent but also because he's simply too unromantic to kick up his heels. . . .

Yet romantic love is, to every normal woman, quite as important as material security and faithfulness. It is, in most cases, the reason she married him in the first place. What man ever won fair maiden by promising, "I will hoe the garden, pay the bills on time and take out life insurance?" No, he pleads, "Darling, I adore you, I want you forever in my arms."

Wrapped in this shining cloak of adoration, she is swept ecstatically into marriage. But, unlike the male of the species, she is not content to drop that cloak and start scrubbing the floor as proof of her corresponding passion. . . .

Note the lack of anecdotes (this time I just didn't need them). And I took care not even to mention my husband. Imagine my shock then when the article was featured on the cover of *Better Homes and Gardens*. This time as "What Became of the Man I Married?" A terrific title, yes, but I was stricken for my husband. It just didn't sound *fair*. He took it like the good sport he was — even the inevitable kidding. But I was devastated. The more mail that poured in the worse I felt. And when it was reprinted in *Reader's Digest* I insisted they label it Anonymous. Ridiculous! I realized later. Who *cares*? Every honest writer who is not ashamed of what he's written should be proud to use his name.

Well, *I* cared. It was mostly to get myself off the hook that I wrote a rebuttal, showing the other side of the coin. I called it, "What Became of the Girl *You* Married?" and used almost the same opening line:

There is one luxury that any man, rich or poor, could give his wife. By the same token, there is one simple yet shining blessing that any woman could bestow upon her husband. It is something that he craves in almost the same measure that she craves attention and affection. . . .

But let's face it. Turning both barrels now upon ourselves, let's admit that many women who bewail their husbands' indifference deserve no better. That with equal justification, countless husbands could compose this ad: *Lost — one gay, sweet bride. Girl who thinks I'm wonderful and tells me so daily and twice on Sundays. Chief characteristic: Appreciation! Ample reward offered by one discouraged guy. . . .*

Both articles brought in an avalanche of mail each time they appeared; first in *Better Homes and Gardens*, then in *Reader's Digest*, including the foreign editions. We actually got letters from all over the world—which only confirms the fact that marriage is a universal fate, often as disturbing to people in Japan or Denmark or Africa, as it may be to the couple next door.

The experience also shows how there are at least two articles in almost every such article, written sincerely from the heart. You simply look at the other side of the question, the opposition's viewpoint, which you have been careful to include, and build it up into a new work to rebut or balance the one you wrote before. This is not hypocrisy or even ambivalence, it is simply playing fair.

It is also very rewarding. Without even meaning to, I did this again, beginning with a lively discourse on a familiar complaint: "Why Men Don't Talk to Their Wives." This article also attracted so many readers I was asked to again flip the coin and portray the other side: "Why Women Can't Talk to Their Husbands."

Herewith a brief sample of style and procedure. First article, opening:

> Nearly every woman I know complains that her husband never tells her anything. I complain right back. Mine doesn't either. If I want to find out anything, I have to depend on the grapevine, I prick up my ears at parties. Then I catch my mate in an unguarded moment and jump him: "Why didn't you tell me the Johnsons are moving, the Blairs are expecting again, and Pete's been promoted? Why don't you ever *tell* me anything?"
>
> Whereupon he will protest that he thought he had informed me of these world-shattering events. And being a woman, I think I've got it figured out why men are so exasperatingly close-mouthed when it comes to their wives. . . .

More serious discussion follows, covering three common areas of difference between men and women; and concludes with a list of our common listening faults: interrupting, woolgathering, difficulty in keeping secrets, etc., each with its bit of explanation.

The second piece opens in similar vein: "If you told the average American man, 'Your wife can't talk to you,' he would think you were out of your mind. 'Talk!' he'd probably explode. 'Why, that's all she does.' " The article continues to explore, again more seriously, the really vital issue, which is communication.

> It's difficult for married people to talk to each other, simply because they know each other so well. One of the glories of courtship is self-revelation. Everything is a matter of marveling. . . . Each rushes to the other to disclose, or discover, some sweet secret of himself. Each thinks, "Ah, at last I'm understood!"
>
> With marriage, however, what was once a voyage of discovery becomes mundane, everyday fare. And the more significant treasures of the spirit get buried in an avalanche of breadwinning, babies and bills. . . .
>
> Because by now the two are strangers. People who may share the same bed and breakfast, but strangers nonetheless. Lovers parted by the very thing they married to get — a life together, understanding.

Both articles suggest a tender compromise. Both have optimistic conclusions.

Note that in all four pieces it was possible to write comfortably from a personal viewpoint, using my own marriage simply as a reference point for the discussion. I have written dozens of articles without including my husband except in the most casual or inferential way. I have also written articles about in-laws without even referring to my own.

There are two very good reasons for this: First, no article is worth hurting or embarrassing anybody, especially people you love. Second, it seems to me in bad taste. There is something offensive about using your own marriage as a good example; and even more offensive about using it as a bad one!

All this is equally true — perhaps even more so, when writing about parents and children.

CHAPTER FIVE

Parents and Children

*T*he subject of your progeny is a highly personal one. As writers we can approach it from two directions:

Parenthood itself.

Advice about raising children.

Here again, a few titles I've used for the first category will illustrate the slant: "A Baby the First Year" (we *had* one, to our astonishment), "Modern Mothers Don't Want Halos," "We Filmed our Baby's Birth" (boy, were some people shocked), "Are You Teacher's Problem Parent?", "What Memories Will They Have of You?", "What Parents Can Do About Obscenity," "If Your Child Runs Away From Home," "Little One Late," (another astonishment, at 40!).

Whether the article is an intensely personal experience — as in the last two titles, or controversial protest — as in the one about obscenity, the subject under discussion is the *adult*. We are analyzing *ourselves*, rather than throwing a spotlight on the children. These are the kind of articles you will find in general circulation magazines, usually far more often than the ones about how to raise children. Of course funny articles about parents and offspring are popular everywhere, and *McCall's* was one of my best markets for sketches and tender, thoughtful essays relating to parents and children. But generally speaking, in this first form the emphasis is on the parents themselves.

In the second — your own discoveries about raising reasonably bright, healthy, happy (and who knows maybe someday very successful?) children, writers face somewhat the same problem as in writing about marriage. Some magazines have their own child care departments, or buy only from a stable of recognized authorities. Some seldom, if ever, use articles on the subject from mere parents. But take heart; those that *do*, don't care *who* writes them, as long as they are well done and have a real contribution to make. In other words, they make sense and are professionally written.

There is also a crop of small magazines aimed at new or expectant mothers and fathers, which welcome their experiences. Some are sponsored by baby-product firms. They don't pay much, but are a good place for beginners to try their wings. Most will send you free sample copies if you ask. So will most of the religious publications, which also use articles from the heart about home and family with an upbeat or spiritual slant. Request a sample and study it before you submit. There are differences in style.

I can't stress too strongly that such publications are the best way to break into print and be paid. Writers with both talent and children can do it if they are willing diligently to try.

How Much Is Fair to Your Family?

Here too you must ask, however, how much of myself and my own family is it good to use? The answer depends upon the kind of article you are writing, and whether or not there is anything in your examples that could possibly hurt your youngster.

Obviously, if you are writing for *Baby Talk*, you can be as personal as you please. The baby couldn't care less! But I think you have to be wary about using your own children, even as the subject of humorous articles. Especially teenagers.

I feel so strongly about this that I once returned a $1,000 check rather than revise an article which the editor wanted me to make "more personal." It was about the tribulations, sometimes hilarious, sometimes anguishing, that beset a family when a boy comes down with "car-itis." I simply could not bring myself to name the boy, and pin his father to the mat; it just was not worth it. (I had written the article in terms of any typical family, using the second person "you." They wanted me to make it 'I' and describe definite events. The article was eventually published, after they compromised.)

I may be unduly sensitive on this point, but I avoid this even with younger children, getting around it in columns and articles by trying never to refer to an actual child by name or age. Substituting "the youngest, the older boy, the middle one, our teenager," or some such term. Also, I almost never use any current, easily recognized example, lest it backfire at school.

Even so innocent an adventure as clumsily trying to help our Bluebird make a blanket roll for camp had repercussions. It seemed harmless and amusing when it appeared. However, the child's well-meaning teacher spied it, and had the mistaken judgment to read it to the class. Our little girl came home in tears: "They laughed at me!" she wailed.

Here your notebook proves invaluable. Write down the anecdotes, situations or problems as they occur, but postpone using them until the child is beyond caring, or sees their value and humor himself. Or at least until you can figure out a way to camouflage them, or use them without upsetting anyone.

For example, at fifteen our son ran away from home. Yes, that "happy home" I was writing about so blithely, where we did all the right things — church, Scouting, fishing trips with Dad, music and merriment with Mother. Yet behind all this was a restless, seeking son. A boy with a very high I.Q., but who hated school, wouldn't study, and simply ran away. Not once but several times! Despite the agony, there were also moments of wry comedy. For instance the time photographers from *Better Homes and Gardens* were coming any minute to illustrate a piece about our joyful family. Except one member was missing; the cab restoring our wandering son was late. They got there before *he* did.

Thank God all this was before the prevalence of drugs and homosexuality; and he was never arrested for anything but hitchhiking. In fact, the authorities who sent him back always complimented us on his honesty and politeness.

Nonetheless, it was a heartrending period for all of us; and it was years before I had the courage to write about it. Mainly because I shrank from the exposure — not so much for myself, but for Jimmy, even though he was now a grown man, accomplished, successful, with a child of his own. Yet one day when we were reminiscing, it was he who actually urged me to tell the story. "Do it, Mother," he insisted. "It could help somebody."

By now I was writing regularly for *Guideposts*, who welcomed the idea. Thinking of Easter and the beautiful analogy that could be made with the empty tomb, I wanted to call it "The Empty Room." Wisely, they urged me to change the title to "A Runaway Son," which would attract more readers. They also advised focusing solely on the initial experience, which was strong enough by itself; I needn't even mention the others. They were right; sometimes less is more. (Editors are not just ogres who reject or ruin your manuscripts. Their advice can be invaluable, no matter how long you have written.)

The article begins with a letter. (When you write from the heart you get a lot of mail.)

"Please pray for Betty," the letter said. "She ran away on her fifteenth birthday a year ago. . . . Will you please pray she's safe and will call us or come home? I can hardly bear to pass that empty room."

That empty room . . . I thought a long time before answering that mother. I went to my files and read similar letters, searching out those that had happy outcomes. . . . I told her about a neighbor's son — and my own.

Because now it can be told. I've been there. I know how it feels to call a child for breakfast, and getting no response, fling open the door–on an empty room. The bedclothes carefully arranged to look like a sleeping figure, but when you pull them back, no sign of the warm body that should be there. The closet mute. The room crammed with his things: books, records, tennis racket, fishing gear; things that should have made him happy, but didn't. All this paraphernalia curiously both a comfort (you tried), and an accusation (you didn't try hard enough).

In those shocked first hours, it isn't the sense of failure that is paramount. There is only this sickening chill in the pit of the stomach. This awful disbelief. He can't be *gone*; there's got to be some mistake! And you get on the phone and call his friends, call the school. And then as the frantic, incredible day drags on into the night, you call the police. *He's threatened, lost, in danger. Find him!*

Such a human drama has the suspense so familiar to parents — lying awake nights praying for a child to get home, even from a date. Keeping vigil, "as if staring out the window into the darkness would somehow produce that precious figure." The endless praying and soul-searching; and the kindness of counselors, teachers, our minister, even the police. These are presented in little vignettes.

But ultimately we must let faith take over. I finally realized this on Good Friday that Easter. Suddenly, in our hushed church, I felt very close to Mary. As if I stood with her on the hillside at Golgotha watching the unspeakable thing happening to her son. . . . But as I wept for her, my own soul was healed and cleansed.

The children didn't understand. They reached out, one on each side of me, to pat and comfort me. And my little girl cuddled near to whisper, "Don't cry, Mommy, Jimmy'll come back."

At that moment faith bloomed. *Hope. Trust.* This was surely the message of the cross—and the empty tomb! When the mother of Jesus was told his tomb was empty, she could release him, knowing God had other plans for her son. He lived and would return!

I could hardly wait to get home to Jimmy's room. Even though he'd been gone for months, I still had been avoiding it. Now I opened the door.

His things were still scattered about, just as he had left them. I began picking them up and putting them away; I cleaned and dusted, getting things ready, making it nice for his return. . . .

•   •   •

Jimmy was restored to us, unscathed. He'd washed dishes, car-hopped, fought forest fires, seen a lot of country. Later, when he was old enough, he joined the Coast Guard, distinguished himself, went on to college. The family was ultimately able to laugh about some of his adventures. But I know how it feels to face an empty room.

Easter has special significance for all parents alarmed about their children. . . . It tells us this is not the end. There *is* hope and life ahead.

There is another reason for waiting to write about such a painful experience. Time gives you perspective. You have grown as a person, and as a writer. You are better prepared to tell the story in a way that will affect the lives of others, knowing their hearts will respond — and as my son said, "It could help somebody."

The mail that poured in proved this over and over. "Now we don't feel so guilty." "You have written our story, almost word for word." "We wept all the way through, because you see, *our* Jimmy never came back. But we were comforted too. Thank you for making it easier."

For me, this is the greatest reward a writer can have.

I have given the example so much space because it is so important.

Don't Kid Yourself by Procrastinating

Now this does not mean you can't *really* write about children until the kids grow up. That's all too common an excuse for procrastination. I have written and sold dozens of child-centered articles with my own all over the place. In fact, there's a family joke: "Mom was always driving us out of her study yelling, 'Beat it, can't you see I'm writing my articles on child psychology?' " I didn't — at least not very often, I couldn't have written without them. But how much to use them depends on the *kind* of article you are writing, and your approach to it.

For instance, "How to Help Your Child Conquer Fear" opened with an anecdote, a daughter's dancing across a footbridge with a harmless green snake coiled around a stick. And *my* impulse to scream and run. But how I overcame it, so as not to inflict my own tormenting snake fears on her. The article then discusses other foolish fears that parents pass along to their offspring; or shows by example how to protect them from such fears:

A child should not only begin life sleeping alone in a darkened room, he should be taught the quiet loveliness of night. My husband used to turn out the lights and sit by a window with our toddler. "We can see the stars better this way. I can just barely see you — can you see me?" he'd laugh. . . . Such happy associations make the dark a friend.

I don't mean to imply that we are model parents on this, or any other, score. It was sheer exasperation over too many nightly trips to the bathroom that inspired us to put a lamp on our daughter's bedside table when she was three. After that, proudly, and without qualms, she turned on her lamp, and trotted down the hall.

The above passage also shows something about tone. You must never sound like a "know-it-all": "We are not model parents. . . . It was sheer exasperation." Note, too, the past tense: "My husband used to. . . . When our child was three." And it seemed in better taste not to specify a name.

A wrong or unfair approach to the same subject might have been handled like this: "Our daughter, Janie, 5, is absolutely terrified of everything that creeps or crawls. She has tantrums, she kicks and screams. I am determined that she overcome this." (Pretty bad, but what I am indicating is that the child is portrayed as the problem, the author as the wise heroine.) Or take the later incident of the dark: "Janie, I am proud to say, turns on her own light when she has to go to the bathroom at night, and marches herself down the hall." To use a child's name, present tense, about this particular function is just — well, not very good judgment.

It is also quite possible, often preferable, to write on these subjects without using your own children at all. Another article of mine, "Help Your Children to Like People," opens:

> The average American parent is eager to give his offspring the so-called advantages. We expose them to dancing lessons, scurry them to the best skin doctors when the bumps of adolescence appear. But too many of us neglect to equip our children with the greatest social advantage of all — the simple, old-fashioned virtue of learning to *like* people.

A number of suggestions follow, enumerated, and presented in statements like: "*Be a good example.* . . . Sons and daughters are but two-legged mirrors of ourselves. *Teach them that friends are worth forgiving.*"

There are all sorts of ways to write beautifully, sensitively, helpfully about children. Again, almost anybody with talent and a loving heart can do it. And in so doing, help other parents who have similar joys and trials but no way to share them. Through the mystery and magic of writing, your voice can be their voice. Your story their story.

This is a contribution all of us should value. When we do we will always have a wide and grateful audience.

CHAPTER SIX
Nostalgia and Memoirs

or me, nostalgia is one of the easiest, most joyful forms of writing. Memories and images from the past just spill out. I suggest nostalgia to anyone who simply wants to write for pleasure, and especially to the person about to write his memoirs.

Nostalgia is not just for senior citizens. If your memories have that universal quality, they will cross generational barriers, whether they are as recent as dear Elvis Presley, or go back as far as mine. Doubleday, my major publisher, rejected *You and I and Yesterday*, saying "Nobody under forty would read it." Quite the contrary, it was the enthusiasm of young people that made it so successful. (And ah, sweet vindication! Many years and printings later, Doubleday bought the rights from Morrow for a trade paperback.) Students at the University of Arkansas chose it for their spring Reader's Theatre production. It was adapted as a play for high schools and churches. And one night, to my delight, I turned on the TV in time to hear a beautiful sixteen-year-old candidate in the *Miss Teenage America* contest doing the last chapter, "Come Home," as a monologue for her talent competition.

Your memories — of the forties, fifties, sixties — are still "the good old days" to *your* generation, with plenty of people around who share them; such memories can also be of interest to children, who want to learn what life was like then. Growing up during the Second World War: Ration coupons and scrap drives, and the awe of seeing a dad or big brother in uniform. Air raid drills at school; the mad celebrations when Japan and Germany surrendered. . . . Scanning the skies for satellites. The first astronauts. The day President Kennedy was shot — what happened at school, at your office, or wherever you were? Everyone seems to remember that tragic time, just as many people remember the day President Roosevelt died. . . .

What, and how much, have things changed, or remained the same? Morals and manners; families and fashions; movies and music; shopping, advertising, transportation; attitudes about life and health and growing old. Because nostalgia, whether in an article or a book, ought to be something more than a picture of the past. I think it should say something about the current scene.

Writing nostalgia is really not hard. But I'll tell you what works for me:

Contrast Present With Past

The strategy I have generally used for articles is to open with a contemporary situation, and contrast it with the past.

For instance, a child at the supermarket exclaiming, "Look, Mommy, vegetables you don't even have to defrost!" . . . And continue, to speak of the time when every backyard had a garden — if you didn't, you were considered either shamefully rich or low-class. I then explore every aspect of the *one phase* of the past I want to recall, and draw some conclusions: "We ate our way through summer, from the crisp carrots to the peanuts we roasted in the bonfires of fall. No competition from junk foods and TV ads; no adult voices urging, 'Now eat your vegetables, take your vitamins.' . . . And, I wish my children could make little boats out of newly picked pea pods, and eat green apples and raid a watermelon patch. . . . Since they can't, I want them to know that fruits and vegetables don't grow on the shelves of a supermarket. That somewhere they are being harvested by human hands, out of God's own earth and sun and sky."

Be Accurate

Whatever the period you are writing about, your memories must be accurate. What games were you playing as kids? Who were the popular movie and TV stars? What songs did you sing? When was the first moon walk — before or after rock became the rage? If in doubt, be sure to check. You don't want readers to catch you in errors. Worse, you don't want to irritate them, as all of us are irritated when we find mistakes in a published piece.

Nostalgic articles (and memoirs, if you decide to write them) do not require a lot of research. They are about as top of the head and deep of the heart as you can get. But when you mention people, places or events, make sure they *could* have been a part of the scene you are recalling for your readers.

Focus on One Topic

I've already mentioned focusing on *one* aspect of the past. For instance (in my own case, at least), the old-fashioned kitchen, children's games, mail-order catalogs, popping corn and making fudge, singing around the piano. Each worthy of a separate piece or chapter, which keeps you from dragging in everything you happen to recall. And always something *specific*, visible, audible, tangible — things which will create vivid pictures for the reader. Never anything so general as "the family," "religion," "friends," or other abstract terms. However, as you describe the various aspects of your subject, you naturally mention the incidental props and people, which also add to the picture of the period. In my "All Doors Led to the Kitchen," for example, the big warm "first family room," the kitchen, is not only furnished in detail, down to the drip pan under the icebox, but we learn something else:

> Hearing the jingle of harness or plod of hooves up the shady street, Mother would open the top lid, make a quick inspection, and send one of us out to tell Johnny Peterson how many pounds today. The Petersons were a big German family who drove teams onto the frozen lake and hewed the ice with giant saws. Their castle-high ice houses were landmarks along the windy shore.
>
> Other kids would already be swarming the hooded wagon, begging bright slivers and chunks to suck. . . . Grabbing a block with the jaws of his mighty tongs, Johnny would haul it toward him and split it cleanly with a pick. . . . Then "slosh" went his bucket of water to rinse the sawdust off, and he'd heave it to his shoulder and stagger, a kind of Atlas, toward the house.
>
> After supper, when the dishes were washed, and the dishpan hung on its nail on the back porch, the family gathered around the kitchen table to eat popcorn and play Flinch, Old Maid or Rummy — although preachers still thundered against "cards" and Mother was uneasy about this wickedness.

The vantage point remains the kitchen, but from it we see other details of a bygone era.

To write this kind of book or article successfully, you need a vivid memory and a colorful style. You don't actually have to believe that the good old days were better, but you should write about them with fondness and good humor. Your object, simply a tender reminiscence of a way of life that is gone. Don't throw it off course by wringing your hands about the problems of today. They will surface, naturally, as you compare and contrast lifestyles, but leave any serious resolutions to the fact writers; or deal with them in your articles of advice or controversy.

For instance, the generation gap — or what to do about grandparents. Here is another example of using the format I suggested. The article opens with a familiar situation: An impending visit from a grandparent and a child saying, "You mean I have to give up my room for a whole *week*?" I then contrast the situation with the past, when grandparents lived with or near their children. The visits to Grandma and Grandpa's house — with its Victrola in the parlor and its wonderful smell of apples, old books and faded velvet draperies. The fun of digging little red new potatoes with Grandpa, and helping Grandma bake sour cream cookies or piece her crazy quilt. Or, when they came to live with us, the comfort of knowing we were always safe and loved just because they were *there*.

Thus I explore *one phase* of the past (the body of the article) before comparing it briefly with life now:

> Today Grandma may still be a chic career woman too busy to bother with grandchildren; someone you call Gigi or Tootsie or just her first name. Both grandparents may have escaped to southern climates, where they live in a condominium or a retirement village, which, except for brief visits, is off-limits to children. Or worse, they may be spending their last days in nursing homes. . . . How much we miss by this separation of the generations. How I wish my children could be as close to their grandparents as I was to mine.

Appeal to a Wide Audience

A nostalgic article cannot be simply the author's egoistic outpourings of his personal reminiscences. Even though written in first person, with points enlivened by anecdotes of friends and family, paradoxically it must not be a mishmash of folksy tales interesting only to the persons involved. It must be sufficiently general to open the gates of memory to others, to make them exclaim, "That's just how it was. Why, I remember — " One of its best rewards is that readers so often write you in this vein, adding wonderful memories of their own.

Despite widely differing backgrounds, there are common bonds among people who enjoy nostalgia. No matter where they live, they are thrilled with what you describe, because they can identify. Somehow, you are telling their stories too. To my surprise I've had letters from Denmark, the British Isles, France; even one from Czechoslovakia exclaiming over how alike we really are: "As children we played almost the same games you did. And my mother washed clothes the same way — she even raced the neighbors to be first to hang them on the line!"

Another important factor is vicarious recognition. The young woman editor who bought *You and I and Yesterday* told me she couldn't resist it, "Because I was born and raised in Manhattan. And I always dreamed of how wonderful it must be to live in a little town."

I'm convinced it was this vicarious thrill that made so many young people take the book to their hearts. Countless letters from them expressed the same theme. Comments from just one, a senior in high school, are typical: "Oh, how I loved those stories of how you grew up in Storm Lake, Iowa! They made me wish I could live in a town like that, with things so much simpler, even though you had it hard. You write such vivid pictures, so beautiful sometimes they made me want to cry. They also make me think more about my own life today, and how different things are. Because we have it hard too, in different ways. I even have a dream that maybe someday I'll be able to write it all down, as you have done, so that other people will know 'how it was then' for *me*!"

I urged that young girl to follow her dream; and to begin preparing for it now, by keeping a journal or notebooks of things she will want to remember later, when she is ready. The same advice is valid for everyone. Your life is important. Write its story. You don't have to be rich or famous — and it doesn't matter where you live. You don't even have to be a Writer. If you have trouble with the actual writing, tell it to a tape recorder, and get somebody to type it for you; and maybe even make corrections or suggestions.

Yes, publication would be nice, but the sad truth is, legitimate publishers seldom risk their money on memoirs; and subsidy (vanity) "publishers" charge enormous sums and do nothing for you. Getting into print, however, is no problem. Simply hire a good printer to print and bind a nice book for you, and circulate it yourself. Poets do this all the time.

Sometimes, although very rarely, a privately printed book will attract so much attention a genuine publisher will want it! But don't worry about anything except telling your story honestly, from the heart, as a lasting record of your life. If it's interesting to *you*, you can make it interesting to other people. Especially those you care most about now, and perhaps generations to follow.

CHAPTER SEVEN

Controversial Topics

*A*rticles of protest or controversy are a natural for almost any writer who does well with the creative from-the-heart form. They are a great way to vent your objections and enthusiasms. And most magazines and newspapers offer outlets for speaking out on controversial subjects. They want not only their readers' opinions, but strong, well-written articles that arouse other people to attack or defend what you say.

Ideas and issues are everywhere, old and new. Even the timeworn question — whether a mother should stay home and raise her children, or park them with other people, to pursue her own career. But whatever you write about, it must have a contemporary slant. (For instance, today the poor gal may *have* to do just that to help meet the bills, and "career" is often a job she hates.) And you must bring to the situation some original points of view.

The situation you are protesting should, of course, be of general interest to other people. (If you're angry at an individual or upset by some personal hurt, write to your diary. If your neighbor's lawn mower maddens you with its noise pollution, especially in the morning, address your local paper.) The subject should be sufficiently familiar and commonly accepted to make your dissenting outcry worth listening to. And you may be surprised at how many readers will come out cheering for you.

Once, infuriated by the violence and explicit sex in movies and on TV, I wrote an article titled, "A Mother Speaks Up for Censorship." I expected to be lambasted; instead, 90 percent of the letters that poured in agreed with me.

Negative and Affirmative

However, you don't have to denounce something to write a strong article. Instead, you can proclaim the joys and rewards of some cause or custom that many other people deplore. To show the contrast—I wrote a very different article, "In Praise of Christmas Letters," with as much fervor, and a lot more fun, than the attack on indecent entertainment.

In both high school and college I debated on teams designated Negative or Affirmative. I can't think of a better way to describe controversial articles. You just take a stand, for or against an issue. Comparison and contrast is an excellent strategy to use in this type of article. You must acknowledge and anticipate the opposition, comparing both sides of an issue, then prove what you are claiming.

I will use those two pieces to illustrate the contrast between them, and show what works, at least for me, in getting your message across.

First, your opening must be strong.

"A Mother Speaks Up for Censorship"

The article starts out swinging:

> As a writer, I never thought the day would come when I'd be asking for censorship. As a parent, however, I'm begging for it—or at least some controls over our mass media of entertainment; yes, and literature. . . . Our children are being brainwashed of the concepts of morality which decent parents still try to teach them. . . . What's more, parents themselves are being subjected to a massive brainwashing. . . . While propaganda for crime, violence and sex bombard our young, parents get nothing but the brute challenge, "It's all up to you. They're your kids. Run this obstacle course if you can—and it's your fault if they go wrong."
>
> Yet is it? How can we protect our children from these influences, and what are we up against?

The piece continues with personal experiences to illustrate. One of them, shepherding a flock of school patrols to a Saturday matinee at our neighborhood theatre, where we'd been promised family entertainment. Only to discover the double feature included a mob tale of murder, drugs and rape, and a sex comedy about college kids on a drunken beach vacation.

Appalled, I confronted the manager. "It was all I could get," he claimed. "I'm sorry but we can't make money without it." This is the attitude that prevails, from the major studios on down. . . . Yet young people *are* influenced by what they read and hear and see. The movies are a powerful teaching force. . . .

In writing controversy, it helps to quote authorities who agree with your position. Their testimony confirms and enhances the importance of what you're saying. Luckily, I knew several prominent educators who did fervently agree, and were happy to be quoted. The article then turns its guns on my own profession:

Today, drunk with our triumphs for "freedom of the press," we are swamped with books replete with four-letter words, perversion and sensuality in every guise. . . . In view of this we can't expect the movies to make nothing but *Pollyanna*. It was the publishers who first set the trend and gave them the material.

But a good protest should be more than sound and fury; it needs some meat on its bones. I now trace the history of censorship during the late twenties, thirties and forties, when Hollywood itself imposed a list of taboos with the Hays and Johnston codes. Far from stifling artistic freedom, these restraints produced the greatest films ever made. Comedy, musicals, cinema masterpieces. A period so rich in entertainment it has become legendary; critics have since labeled it 'The Golden Age of Movies.'

The article continues with predictions as to what will happen if we don't stop *now*, before this cancer of sex and violence invades our homes through our television sets. And concludes almost as it began:

As for censorship, I'm for it. Even as a writer I'm for it. When people who practice my profession can't make a living without dwelling on the sensational, the salacious, the stuff that will make a hot book jacket and a seductive movie ad, then I say please, somebody step in!

A strong conclusion is vital to a successful protest article. And a good strong conclusion usually contains three things: It ties directly to the opening, restates your conviction, and challenges the reader to *do* something himself.

Publication

Short creative articles don't usually need query letters. But a longer article of such consequence does justify such an inquiry before sending it out. To my amazement, three major markets declined this one, as being *too* controversial. They were afraid of their readers' reaction (likewise advertisers', I suspect) to the very word *censorship*. Only faithful *Today's Health*, published by the AMA, had the courage to print it. But they did so proudly; it was widely reprinted, and suddenly I became a controversial figure myself. Torrents of mail poured in, calling me everything from a Communist to a saint. I was invited to appear on local talk shows, speak at churches and clubs; and even to testify before a Congressional committee, which was finally investigating obscenity laws.

They were trying to decide whether it might be better to legalize pornography, like the Scandinavian countries; and/or adopt a movie rating system like the British. This last step I advised. Foolishly, I realized later. Ratings don't keep anybody *out*, they only lure more people in. The worse the ratings the bigger the box office draw.

The article was also the subject of discussion on a then very popular Sunday night prime-time TV program: The David Susskind Show. Nobody warned me. It was already on the air when people began calling me to urge, "Tune in, they're talking about *you!*" An impressive panel — Gore Vidal, producer Otto Preminger, a psychiatrist, another famous writer, and a Catholic priest. And what a great time they had mocking and scolding "that little Washington housewife," so scared her children were being corrupted that she would attack our Constitutional rights to freedom of expression, and shackle all arts by the grim Gestapo of *censorship*.

Only the psychiatrist spoke in my defense. "She's right about one thing — our obsession with sex. That's the first symptom I notice in a really sick patient. A nation obsessed with sex is *sick*."

The books and films I was deploring are like Sunday School stories compared to what we see today. But I'm glad that as a writer I could take a stand. You don't always win your battles, but it's good to know you *fought*.

"In Praise of Christmas Letters"

This article too was longer than most—about 2,500 words. Enthusiastic applause for something others may boo, but you find good, deserves equal space. And emotionally it's great; you don't have to get mad (leave that to the critics), just cheer whatever you honestly enjoy, and give your reasons.

Like its predecessor, the piece states its premise, confronts the opposition head-on, and proceeds to prove its case (three elements that are important to a strong opening).

> Deck the halls with boughs of holly, 'tis the season to be jolly! I'm about to write our family Christmas letter . . . and frankly, I can hardly wait.
>
> Never mind that Christmas letters have gotten a bad press lately. "Brag sheets" they've been called. "Boring reports that nobody reads." Well, let the scoffers scoff, the Scrooges sneer. To me, the annual exchange of these letters is one of the happiest customs to appear on the American scene. A song of hope and joy in this troubled world, proclaiming that despite the trials that beset us, each year of life is to be treasured. God is good!
>
> Christmas letters also serve two useful purposes. The can forge a vital link between friends who don't want to lose each other. And your own letters, if you save them, will provide a record for your family, each one a small but shining chapter in its biography.

The article continues with the story of how we came to write them, and what these "adventures in living" have meant to us and our friends over the years. It then enhances an important point:

> But quite apart from other people's reactions to your Christmas letter, the truth is, you're not writing them for other people, *you are writing them for yourself*. Harvesting these memories for the sheer joy of hugging them to your heart again, fixing them in time. . . . And

they will be a rich harvest of memories for your family. Your Christmas letters can become their history. . . . One-sided, yes, leaving out most of the troubles, but important in their statement that no matter what else may have happened during those difficult years, our life together was good. . . .

After more personal illustrations and discussion, the article concludes:

That first Christmas, the angel proclaimed the birth of Jesus saying, "I bring you good tidings of great joy, which shall be to all people!" Our Christmas letters are our hearts' carols proclaiming, "Joy to the world! We've made it through another year and life is good!"

Surely this is a beautiful thing.

The Writer's Reward

The controversial article is very rewarding to a writer. The audience is vast, whether your approach to an issue is pro or con. It's wonderful to know your voice will be heard. In this, perhaps as in no other form, your opinions will matter. Because you are expressing the feelings and convictions of a great many people who have neither the voice nor the platform to express it themselves.

For me, this is one of a writer's best rewards.

CHAPTER EIGHT

Advice and Self-Help

dvice wears many faces. It's hard to write about love and marriage and children, or almost anything else without it. Even if you're not doing so on purpose, advice is evident, if only implied. Advice even makes its way into true stories of personal adventure sometimes: for instance, once I wrote about getting stranded alone one night on the Mexican border with a flat tire, and floodwaters lapping at my feet. An alarming situation, made worse by my anxiety about the strange men who stopped to help. "They told me I was also out of gas; I had no choice but to go with them."

The drama was fraught with impending danger. No advice was necessary—it was flagrant from the opening line describing how I set off alone to meet my husband, knowing the flood was rising, and without even checking my gas or tires. (*Don't be stupid, take somebody with you, be sure you can get there safely.*) Luckily, the adventure turned out all right.

But Self-Help articles, as we call them, are definite articles of advice addressed to readers, in which you share what you think about overcoming obstacles and improving the quality of life. Ideas which could also help them. Don't worry about your qualifications. Giving advice is as normal as breathing. Everybody does it all the time. Parents, neighbors, relatives, friends. You just do it better if you can write.

Your titles convey the topics. A few from my ample stock: "Put Your Worries to Work," "Kill That Can't Complex," "I'm Going to Unclutter My Life," "Keep Your Husband in Your Arms," "Don't Be Afraid to Be a Friend."

This last advice applies to *you* as you write. Your style and tone should be warm and friendly. Convincing, yes, but never preachy, teachy or authoritative ("do this because I say so!"). But rather the voice of someone the reader will enjoy and trust. Someone he or she might like to have lunch with.

Advice articles aren't hard to write once you get the hang of them. Again, the best way to learn is to read them, picking up this *style and tone* and analyzing *how they are put together*. I believe that therein lies the entire secret of successful articles of advice: Style; and organization. Each has a separate chapter in Section II of this book. For now, I will illustrate with excerpts from two articles.

The first, a Marriage Article *designed* to give advice.

"Keep Your Husband in Your Arms," opens with an anecdote:

> You've taken a last look at the pot roast, turned the fire lower, and consulted the clock when the telephone rings. It's your husband announcing, "I won't be home for dinner, dear. I've got to work late. . . ." If you're like one of my friends, Ellen, you'll immediately suspect he's lying. But if you're like most wives, you may scold, "Darn it, why didn't you warn me earlier?" Or you may worry, "Dear, you really shouldn't, you're already tired. . . ."
>
> The difference is this: Ellen is one of those few women who cannot trust their husbands. For she has been hurt by the bitter experience of infidelity. You, and thousands like you, are the typical lucky ones, married to the fundamentally faithful, home-loving, hardworking, average American guy. . . . Oh, I know what Kinsey says about him . . . yet I think the erotic label is a gross distortion of today's average husband. I believe that a man blessed with a healthy personality, a happy home, and the right sort of wife doesn't *want* to stray.

The anecdote sets the scene, the above paragraph states the premise — which should be established early. (What am I trying to prove? What is this article all *about*?) I then give four reasons why most men would rather stay safely at home with their wives than play around. And proceed to draw the "Portrait of a Perfect Wife." Consisting of eight qualities that will keep her husband in her arms. From simply making him comfortable, to caring enough about him to fight for him should the threat arise. "She may not only save her home, but save her husband for everything he holds dearest.''

These qualities form the body of the article, which concludes: "The woman who keeps her husband in her arms learns to be both sweetheart and companion.''

The article appeared in *Family Circle*, where it brought in a lot of mail, and was widely reprinted.

There are other ways to present advice, as you will see in chapter 13. But this format is so effective I've used it often, with variations to fit the material. I want to demonstrate how it was adapted to another piece, titled "Twelve Steps to Self-Confidence," written for *Nation's Business*, as I recall. Later it was published as a booklet for the Good Reading Rack Service. The editors helped by providing a subtitle, "Who's Really Self-Confident?" to introduce the opening scene:

> A train speeds toward a small Midwestern town. On the platform awaiting its arrival is the president of the Kiwanis Club, with a committee of businessmen. "Boy, what a lucky, self-confident guy Jim is," one of them thinks about the president. "What wouldn't I give to have a personality like that?" For he cannot know that behind that jovial smile and hearty manner Jim is in knots of anxiety:
>
> *What will he say to the prominent person they have come to meet?* he worries. *Mustn't sound too corny, big shot from the city like that . . . what if he goofs? The club will be embarrassed, see what a mistake they made in electing him. . . .*
>
> Meanwhile, on the train the visiting speaker sits perspiring. The nearer he gets to his destination the more nervous he feels:
>
> *Silly, after all the speeches he's made — but will his talk go over?* He reads through his notes again, making last minute changes . . . and notices, to his horror, a button dangling on his sleeve. *Too late to fix, and why did he ever wear this jacket? What a sloppy impression he'll make! . . . As for his speech — SUCCESS.* He writhes, *sometimes it seems like a cruel joke. Sure, he's gone pretty far, made a lot of money, but his ambitions were so much higher. You phony!* he thinks. . . .
>
> The train stops. The man on the platform leaps forward and

extends a hand to grasp that of the man descending. Both are smiling, the handshake is firm. Now that the moment has arrived and they find themselves in action, sheer habit rescues them. They say the right things. Both have begun to relax, to realize there is nothing to fear in the situation.

In short, self-confidence — like money — is something we think everybody else has but us. Yet feeling shy and insecure is perhaps the most common of human afflictions.

The piece now quotes three famous people who suffered from feelings of inferiority, then presents the list of twelve ways to overcome it, as promised in the title, each one with a brief discussion and example.

1. **Grow up!**

Wean the child within you. Remember, you are no longer that forlorn little girl who wasn't asked to the party, or that kid who failed to make the team.

2. **Do the thing you dread.**

Jim Beal dreaded facing the important stranger. The speaker was equally filled with doubts and dread. Yet each knew the honor was worth the misery.

3. **Be prepared.** The Boy Scouts are right. Self-confidence comes a lot easier to the person who's sure he's ready.

4. **Be careful of your grooming.**

No matter how well-prepared, self-confidence can be shaken by the discovery of a spot on your tie or a runner in your stocking.

5. **Accept the physical You — or change it!**

A very important part of self-confidence is self-acceptance. Especially of the physical package.

6. **Act the part.**

There is a bit of an actor in everyone who radiates self-confidence.

7. **Learn to speak effectively.**

Some people are born with "the gift of gab," a lot of us have to learn it. Here are some suggestions. . . .

8. **Be a good listener.**

The person of composure realizes it's just as important to listen.

9. **Become an interesting person.**

Read, learn, go places, see and do interesting things. The more interesting you know yourself to be, the more confidence you'll have with other people.

10. **Learn to like yourself.**

Don't be too hard on yourself, and never downgrade yourself to others. Be thankful for what attributes you have, and make the most of them.

11. **Remember, you are not Exhibit A.**

It is said of animals, "They're more scared of us than we are of them." This applies as well to people. . . . Take it easy, enjoy yourself, you are not the center of attention.

12. **Put other people at ease.**

Introduce yourself to that stranger in the crowd. Invite the newcomer at work to lunch. . . . By going into action your own restraints and self-consciousness are dissolved. . . . The best way to achieve true poise is to start thinking of others.

Every one of those twelve steps could be the subject of a full-blown article. In fact, I did so with "Do the Thing You Dread," and several others, by simply expanding the brief discussions which accompanied their listings.

It's never hard to find ideas for such articles from the heart. Once you get in the habit of doing them, they pop up like dandelions, and multiply so profusely, it's hard to stop.

CHAPTER NINE

Humor

I come from a family of kidders, jokers and tellers of funny stories. We didn't have much money, but laughter, "like a good medicine," as the Bible says, pulled us through the tough times and enriched our lives. Things often got so hilarious at the table, somebody had to be excused. Mother and my sister Gwen were very witty, Dad and my brothers born entertainers. I was more serious. All this laughter delighted my soul, but I was more likely to dart from the table and try to scribble some of their high jinks down.

As a grown-up writer I didn't specialize in humor, although I've published quite a few things in that vein. And humor keeps popping up in my articles, whatever their type. A touch of humor is just one of those little extras that brighten almost anything you write, and help it sell. In this chapter we'll discuss both uses of that delightful and valuable tool. And we'll start by pointing out a few no-no's to avoid, whether you're writing an article meant solely to be funny, or just attempting to add that extra bonus to an otherwise serious piece.

First, *don't* ever use an old joke (or even one currently making the rounds) under the impression that this is humorous writing. Occasionally even good writers who should know better are guilty of such attempts to be funny, and I always wince for them. There is something about the very word or framework of a "joke" when reduced to print, which makes it suddenly dead. But a joking or kidding *attitude* toward your material is something else. You are personally amused by it as you write, and that amusement shines through.

But never strain for effect. This humor must come naturally, otherwise the strain will show. Your article will become self-consciously cute or embarrassing. It will make the reader feel like the wife who has to sit politely smiling while her husband prances around in a lady's hat, or lengthily tells a not very funny story. Or like the class that sits groaning while their staid professor tosses off an old chestnut.

On the positive side: *be original*. This is especially important if you're writing the humorous article per se. Even the titles should have a fresh and comic bounce. Which really isn't hard. Just take a usable pun or familiar saying, and change its meaning by giving it an original twist. Then exaggerate the situation, with a touch of self-satire.

Here, for example, are a couple I did for the Sunday supplements.

"*Don't* You Be My Valentine." (A mother's frenzied last-minute efforts to help her children get ready for Valentine's Day the night before.) Which begins:

> The encyclopedia says that three different martyrs have feast days on February 14 — and that's how come we have valentines. I think any mother would agree that they've got the *wrong martyrs*. Or that if they could figure out which one really started the valentine bit he'd never have been made a saint!

"Flowers in My Hair," (again using exaggeration) tells how the dandelions and other wild things in our first yard were doing beautifully, to our delight — until zealous neighbors with ten green thumbs descended upon us, bearing gifts of seeds and bulbs and seemingly more suitable plants. Which I didn't know what to do with. And worse, didn't care to learn. I just didn't *want* to raise flowers!

Even if you are writing a serious article, it sometimes helps to choose original analogies and allusions which will give it a comic bounce. For instance, when writing about the bad influence immoral movies may have on young people and the paltry defenses of the public against them, I stated, "Attempting to combat the sex tycoons with such weapons is like aiming a pea shooter at a bull elephant." I tried several images before that one struck me. It was just ludicrous enough to say what I intended.

Here's an example from "Marriage Isn't a Reform School": "Kiss the girl or boy of your dreams goodbye. You're not married to Clark Gable or Marilyn Monroe, you're married to just plain Bill or Jane Jones." (That shows how long ago that article was written. If it hadn't sold and I was trying to revise it, I would choose current entertainers; even in love symbols, styles change.)

And, again, from "Do You Dare to Be Honest in Marriage?": "Practically all wives fudge a little when it comes to what they pay for things." (I'm using intentional vernacular, bordering on cliché, here, to make it all sound very homey and everyday.) "What woman in her right mind ever admits to buying a dress that wasn't marked down? And it's sheer unconscious feminine psychology to add anything from $10 to $50 to what it was marked down *from*. Any man who has any wits about him at all knows she does this, comes to expect it, and almost certainly would be faintly shocked if she didn't."

This is not outright humor. But it's humorous in attitude, in tone. It bespeaks a cheerful approach to a subject that might well have been treated with dead seriousness, and is, in other places in the article. It is the light treatment that editors like.

You must be careful, however, that your light or comic touches occur in just the right places, and do not spoil that so very important tone. Here is an example of misplaced, woefully inappropriate humor from a manuscript:

> These thugs attacked without provocation, they were suddenly upon me and I was fighting for my very life. Their blows rained down, they were trying to stamp upon me. "Father forgive them," I prayed even in that moment. And I was in dead earnest, in fact I was nearly dead, Ernest, as my brother used to quip.

The reader, like the victim, rolls his eyes to heaven. It is not only an antique joke, but is worse — it injects a screechingly wrong note.

Timing and Beat

Timing is tremendously important. One of my brothers was in show business, and I learned from him how comics must develop a perfect sense of timing: The pause before the punch line, the quick pickup, the delicate balance between getting a laugh and laying an egg.

This timing, this complete command of pace, is especially important to the writer, whether he's writing straight humor or material that is humorous in approach. He must phrase and rephrase, add and subtract, until the episode or reference balances out to achieve its funniest impact. In most instances it is the subtracting that helps most. The wisecrack *must* crack—and then quit right there. The anecdote cannot lumber on for pages. Pare the dialogue until every line is funny, or leads into the next line, which will be. Avoid pointless chatter like this:

"I don't like this," said my wife, pouting.

"Well, it can't be helped, honey," I told her, grinning slyly.

"It can too. You could do something about it if you would. I declare I never knew anybody to be so contrary. Why, sometimes I think you haven't a brain in your head."

"Oh, come now, you don't think that, you can't, after all you married me. Now let's see what we can do."

On and on, wasting the reader's time until finally a bright line is painfully squeezed out.

On the other hand, it is the deft, subtle little balances of "he said," or "the child remarked, grinning up at me," that give your comedy the exact *beat*, the pace, the timing to amuse the mental ear. A good way to test yourself about this is to try to write some anecdotes for the various departments in *Reader's Digest*. Read yours aloud, and then read their published ones aloud, and *listen*. See how yours compare. It is not easy to compress an experience into a paragraph or to combine a few words in a way that packs a wallop.

Genuine humorists usually have this intuitive sense of timing. This is why stand-up comedians can tell a joke and have the audience in tears of laughter, while the less gifted may tell the same story and have people groaning. Those who have to labor to be the life of the party usually aren't. But writing humor also requires work and practice. The writers don't just take dictation from gag writers, but may rewrite a situation or revise a sentence half a dozen times before it feels or sounds right.

Logic

Oddly enough, humor, which depends so frequently upon hyperbole, has its own stubborn logic. It must be based upon reason and reality, life as we actually know it to be. The contrast may be one of the psychological reasons it strikes us funny.

Let me try to make this clear: A long time ago, when my efforts to make money through writing included soap contests, limericks and light verse, I also wrote gag lines for a cartoonist. One, I blush to admit, suggested an escaped convict at a fancy party, saying, "Oh, yes, I'm sought after everywhere." The artist shot it back with this comment: "If he were being sought by the police, he could not possibly be at this party. Be logical—humor is based on logic."

I never forgot that advice. The more logical, the more reasonable the humorist is, the funnier his flights of exaggeration. You know he's kidding, but somewhere down below his wildest fancies lies this hard core of truth.

The would-be humorist often isn't logical. He seems to think that sheer unmotivated nuttiness is enough. I recently read a book-length manuscript for a publisher in which the basic setup could have been insanely funny. The treatment made it merely insane. In addition to many other defects, it lacked this essential logic. The hero was determined to operate a very unusual business from the White House. (In fairness to the author and his excellent idea I won't tell you what it was.) Complication piled upon ludicrous complication. Yet it was never clearly established how the man and his family actually got there, or what their motivations were. Most of the comedy collapses because it has no logical foundation, even in basic character. The reader keeps wondering how the incidents *could* be happening in the first place, and since this is never revealed, credibility is destroyed. They just couldn't have happened that way.

Here we see again how closely the creative article writer is kin to the fiction writer. Particularly the humorist. Whether writing a short piece for *The New Yorker*, or any popular magazine, or a funny book, he must understand what motivates human behavior; his characters must be soundly conceived. Then when they behave in a strange fashion the reader will know why, and his credulity will not be strained.

Hyperbole

Hyperbole, or the art of exaggeration, is the humorist's meat. He takes a perfectly plausible situation and blows it to preposterous proportions. Or he takes some fantastic possibility and makes it seem ridiculously reasonable.

You will recognize in all successful hyperbole a basis of absolute logic and truth. That's exactly what makes it so funny. From this base of all too familiar experience, we love to be catapulted into its extremes.

A word of caution, however. Hyperbole is not to be confused with hysteria. Verbs of intense emotion or exaggerated action do not in themselves make humor; such words as "scream," "stamp," "smirk," "leer," etc. are to be used sparingly.

Self-Satire

A staple on the shelves of humor is the article of self-satire. You simply take some foible, weakness, or other aspect of your own personality and make fun of it. Usually something which is very familiar to your reader.

> I'm a lid loser. Every jar, jug, tube or bottle in my kitchen always stands decapitated. Because whenever I open anything, the lid disappears the minute I turn my back. Never to be found again, no matter how feverishly I look. *That* lid for that container has simply vanished (maybe with some other rebel runaway lid) forever. Oddly, other lids of various shapes and sizes pop up all over the place. Which I hopefully capture, and stow away in a special drawer, just in case. . . . But in vain. Because *never* in the history of my housekeeping has one of those lids *ever* fit anything I needed it for.

But you don't always have to exaggerate. Sometimes the true stories of our human peccadillos can be just as entertaining. Witness the followup to that particular piece in my "Love and Laughter" newspaper column:

> I also lose glasses. Once, on a trip to Europe, I broke a pair, lost a pair, and borrowed a pair to read with flying back — then left them on the plane! As soon as possible, I hurried to my optician to have

some more made. But we got to talking, and when I got home the phone was ringing. It was my friend the oculist saying, "You forgot your glasses!"

Months later, in mountains 500 miles away, my husband and I were having dinner at a revolving restaurant. But my glasses disappeared the minute we sat down. He had to read the menu to me. As we finished, I saw a familiar face beaming and waving something across the room. Then he hastened to our table; to my astonishment, it was my pal the optician.

"What are *you* doing here?" I gasped.

"I must have known you'd need me," he grinned. "The first time these went by, I thought they looked familiar. The second time I had a hunch. The third time I grabbed them, telling my wife *Marjorie Holmes*. She's *got* to be here. She's the only gal I know with traveling glasses."

Proudly, he handed them over. "Once again I have the pleasure. Here's your glasses."

This sort of thing looks easy. It isn't. You have to be so careful of every word, for timing and pace. And there is the ever-present danger of straining for effect, or of sounding just too, too cute. Once you turn the spotlight on yourself, even in a manner meant to be unflattering, the audience expects you to be very entertaining indeed to compensate for the attention you're getting. This is the trouble with many amateur attempts. When coyness is substituted for cleverness, the result is only embarrassing:

I'll betcha you're beginning to think I'm just about the worst steno' in the world. Well, I betcha you could just about be right, on account of I could hardly barely get through shorthand, and my typing, goodness! As for spelling, silly as it may sound, sometimes I can't really remember how to spell my own name. Well, but this boss (poor man) decided to take a chance (he was sooo good looking too) maybe because I batted my new false eyelashes at him.

Goodness!

Some General Guidelines

Here are some things to aim for and to watch out for in writing humor, plus a few more suggestions.

1. Be original—don't fall back on old situations, gags or jokes.

2. Never make less fortunate individuals the butt of laughter.

3. Be careful not to inject humor at the wrong place or in the wrong context.

4. Watch your timing. There must be a brisk, lively beat.

5. Don't substitute hysteria for hyperbole. (Be wary of such verbs as "stamped," "screamed," "bellowed," "whimpered," "moaned," etc.)

6. Watch your tone.

7. Never inject negatives such as: "I know this isn't very funny." (If it isn't, the reader won't have to be told.) Or, in the manner of some TV comedians whom I promptly turn off: "Boy, did that lay an egg," or "Who wrote this terrible script, anyhow?"

8. Never exhort the reader: "Boy, did I laugh," or "It was absolutely rib-splitting," or "Tears of laughter rolled down our cheeks." Humor cannot be described or discussed, it must come from the writing itself.

9. Watch out for *italics*, CAPITAL LETTERS, exclamation points!! Lavish or frantic punctuation cannot compensate for lack of cleverness.

10. Bright or witty effects can be achieved through: puns; cliché twists; a play on words; use of opposites; specifics.

11. Be very careful of slang and swearing.

Some writers have the impression that a subject is made funny by mere breeziness of style. To achieve this breeziness they lean heavily on slang. Phrases such as, "Man, oh, man—," "Sez who? Sez me," "Oh yeah?" etc. Or they inject totally meaningless asides intended to convey some mood of humor. "Still do" (make these mistakes), or "still am" (trying to learn better), "Well, you never know," "Could be," "It just goes to show—"

Sometimes, to add to the slam-bang effect, they throw in swearing: "It was really one helluva situation." "What do you do in a case like that, for Chrissake?" Or they sprinkle oaths through the dialogue. Perhaps they do this because they have *heard* some very funny individuals talk that way. But live, "in-person" comedy is always generated as much by the personality of the comedian himself as by the things he says. You simply cannot capture this and make it funny on paper. It only gets bombastic, noisy, dull—and is sometimes in bad taste.

12. Don't depend upon things or situations too obviously *expected* to be funny (the antics of a monkey, for instance, a man's bald head, a woman's girdle, losing your undies on the street). The late syndicated columnist George Dixon once wrote a piece on humor in which he said: "The trouble is that the broader the absurdity, the harder it is to make it come out funny on paper" adding that the two principal ingredients of humor are recognition and surprise.

This relates right back to two principles of any good article from the heart: identification and hope or promise. When we go a step further, when the ordinary, the logical, are exaggerated or so twisted about that they become astonishing or highly unusual, then something in the reader responds—he is amused. Thus we achieve humor, whether a piece is funny in its entirety, or merely amusing in spots or in general tone.

CHAPTER TEN

Essays, Sketches and Columns

*E*ssays, sketches and columns are like members of an intriguing family. Their differences so slight it's sometimes hard to tell them apart. Essays are usually a little longer and more thoughtful; sketches shorter and lighter in tone — much as an artist sketches his scene. For me sketches are the easiest, most enjoyable form of writing — thanks, once again, to the habit of keeping notebooks and journals, where ideas, emotions and images spill out just because you can't bear *not* to write them. Also, I started out as a poet. I think most truly creative writers do. The music of words — their sound and cadences are seldom silent in your head. And this mysterious dance and song of language, almost begging to be captured, is what also makes your prose appealing. Even poetic.

The sketch or essay requires no special form. You simply dip into your own memories or daily activities and discover one moment, statement, action or object which seems to epitomize some universal truth. It may be based on a phrase that impressed you, an epigram or bit of philosophy which expresses some human wisdom for you in capsule form. Anything so simple as a mother's constant reminder, "Shut the door!" which I turned into "Shut Those Doors Behind You" (on regret, missed opportunities, etc.) for *McCall's*. Or the familiar shout, "Mother, I'm home!" Tracing it from kindergarten through college, into your children's marriages. In part:

> They grow up so fast; they go away one by one. After a while, only on visits does that glad cry come. . . . Home is somewhere else. A different job, a different life, a different love to follow yours, a different person to greet them when they return. . . .

And that once-familiar cry has taken on a new significance. . . . You don't have to worry. They have reached their destination. Each one is safely in. In a new and much more wonderful way each voice is assuring you: "I'm home, Mother. I'm *home!*"

In most of my magazine pieces (particularly those for *McCall's*), and later in my newspaper columns, I also used familiar objects as symbols to clarify simple truths: a tent, a table, the flag on the schoolhouse, the family calendar, a father's wallet. Here, for instance, are the opening and closing paragraphs from "Dad, I Need Some Money" (*McCall's*):

> To me, one of the most touching gestures a man makes is that old familiar one of reaching into his hip pocket and drawing forth his wallet. . . .
> "Dad, I need some money." How many billfolds that plea wears out! No wonder husbands so often need new ones. . . . The wallets get tired and worn and thin; eventually, they give up.
> But the men? Tired and worn though they too may become, somehow they can't just quit, and they seldom give up. They are made of tougher, finer leather, sewed with sinews much too stong. So long as there's life in their bodies and love in their hearts and somebody to say, "Dad, I need some money," they manage to keep on filling their wallets.
> And reaching for them.

The entire essay is based upon a single analogy or bit of symbolism which is its own memory device. Thus unity is inherent; and with one incisive theme, you achieve one mood or tone, and one final effect. Sometimes it is written entirely in the first person, sometimes you step back a few paces to use the third person, or you may concentrate on the second person, "you." But the feeling is always first person, in other words, intimate.

The writing must be clear, pure, succinct. Sentiment is always present, but sentimentality, never. Once you spill over into clichés (Father's "care-worn hands," etc.) or anything that smacks of hearts and flowers, you're ruined. The writing must not only "give pleasure" (which Virginia Woolf considered one of the basic principles of the essay), it must have a certain timelessness: "A good essay must have this permanent quality about it; it must draw its curtain round us, but it must be a curtain that shuts us in, not out."

The only earthly way to learn to write essays is to write them! Don't strive for perfection at first; just pour your essay ideas into your notebook as they come to you, and let them age a bit. Meanwhile, study the published essays to soak up their flavor, their rhythms, their delicate balance of ideas, emotion and phrase. Then go back to your own earlier sketches and polish until they shine.

The Newspaper Column

I was already contributing to most of the magazines, and had published three novels before deciding to try a newspaper column. It proved to be the luckiest, most rewarding step of my writing life.

Like most of us, I had always had the urge to write a column and felt sure I could. But not until I was going through some of my old notebooks one summer day at our lakeside cabin, did I *know* it had to be done — if only to use this treasury of material. The times I had already dipped into it for articles and stories, barely made a dent. On and on I read: copious notes about the children, word pictures, prose poems, philosophy, imagery, bright sayings, family adventures, all poignant and tender and funny.

Why, this is some of my best writing, I realized. Did all this come out of *me*? I rejoiced, but I also wanted to weep. Only another writer can understand the ache that follows on making such a discovery of your own work later. Or the anguished question: *How can you let it go to waste?* And, like an answer, those long ago words of Dewey Deal began echoing in my head: "Write beautiful things for people who crave beautiful things. There is a *duty*."

For a time I stared into the distance, taking stock. Then I sprang up and went rummaging for the copy of *Writer's Digest* I'd been saving, with a wonderful article giving specific advice about columns. (How I wish I could thank the author.)

Columns should be about 600 words, I learned. Prepare five or six examples and submit with a query letter including your credits. Get a personal interview with the editor, if possible. Start with the most likely paper in your present hometown.

Our home at that time was Washington, D.C. The major dailies were *The Washington Post* and *The Evening Star*. One of my best friends, who wrote a society column for the *Post*, told me to forget it. "It's too tough to break in; reporters would *kill* for a column, and editors hate newcomers. Besides, I'm afraid Washington is too sophisticated for anything home-spun."

She had a point — but so did I. Both papers had columns and features aplenty about embassy parties, dinners at the White House, and the daz-zling doings of diplomats, celebrities, and famous hostesses; but nothing beyond recipes, "Dear Anns," and household hints for the average wife and mother who seldom gets near such events. This seemed to me a plus.

My friend was right about getting rebuffed, however. When I worked up the nerve to call the *Post*, the women's editor made short work of me. "No *thank* you!" she snapped as I attempted to describe my reason for an interview. "We already have more columns now than we *need*." And hung up.

I raged a minute. Then, wiping my eyes and gritting my teeth, I called the switchboard at the *Star* (I didn't even know the name of the women's editor). She was Lee Walsh, they told me, and she sounded even tougher, but when I called, at least she listened. Then: *No* Flatly. She was too busy to see me, and there was simply no space for another column. "However, if you care to come in — I probably won't be there, just leave a few on my desk." Bang! down went another receiver.

Stung, I cried some more. Why *bother*? It was a long way into the city; and she might not even *be* there. Why risk more humiliation? My time was too valuable to waste. . . . However . . . how-*ever* — the word kept taunting me. No matter how condescending, *however* also means *maybe*, a flicker of hope, a crack in the door. And writers can't afford hurt pride. The next day, dreading it, I set off, stubbornly carrying twelve columns instead of six, and a brief bio in case she wasn't available.

The editor was there, after all — I was directed to her desk. She was easy to spot across the room, very imposing, very much the boss, in an enormous hat. Absently, she motioned me to a chair while she finished her phone conversation; then without a word picked up my sheaf of papers and began to read. First, the letter, which seemed to surprise her; then very swiftly, the first two columns. She paused to regard me a moment before flipping briskly through the rest. Suddenly, putting them down, she faced me squarely and asked, "How much do you want for these?"

I gasped. I had not prepared for this. But from some hidden reserve of poise, I heard my voice saying pleasantly, "My goal is syndication. I'm sure rates can be arranged."

To my further astonishment, Mrs. Walsh got to her feet, holding out her hand. She was actually smiling, and her handshake was warm. "I want to show these to my managing editor," she said. "We'll be in touch. *Thank you* for thinking of the *Star*!"

Blissfully, not quite believing , I sort of floated out of that ancient red-brick building, with its clatter of presses and hurrying feet, its rich, exciting smell of old wood and ink. (*The Evening Star* was one of the first dailies in America.) Still in a dream, I drifted home to wait . . . and wait. By the third week, I was desperate. Nervously, fearing the worst, and hating to intrude, I finally dialed.

Lee Walsh herself answered. "Thank goodness!" she exclaimed. "We've been trying to reach you." (Stupidly, I'd forgotten to leave my phone number, which was in my husband's name.) "Mr. Hill *loves* your column, we want to get started right away. How soon can you come in?"

The managing editor met me in the corridor, arms outspread, a tall, slim, gray-haired man with the keenest, sweetest eyes in the world — or so it seemed. He practically hugged me into his office where Mrs. Walsh was waiting. "It's warm, it's human, it has *heart*! Can you be ready by Easter? We'll launch it then."

We worked out the details that afternoon. They had chosen "Love and Laughter," from my list of suggested titles. To appear twice a week, Sundays and Wednesdays.

Only one thing seemed to bother Bill Hill. "How soon will you run dry?"

I laughed. "Never!" I told him. "I'm a bottomless pit."

The Format

My usual pattern was this: An opening sketch, essay or personal story, followed by various subheads or categories: "Dialogues With a Daughter," "Moments That Make Marriage Worthwhile," "Tales That Touch the Heart," "My Favorite Neighbor Says," "Beauty in Your Own Backyard," "The Small Fry Say." And others. I often ended the column with "Apron Pocket Prayers" (which proved very popular) or "Lyrics for Everyday Living" (my own verse, and that of readers). The category titles were flexible, and sometimes appropriate for the opening sketch.

Bill Hill was particularly enthusiastic about these categories. "They're like appetizers to the meal, or side dishes that give it flavor and lead the reader on. It's so easy to lose the reader; most people don't even finish a single-subject column."

In describing personal experiences, I used present tense. And instead of the editorial "we," which I dislike, or "I" and "ours," which sounds to me—well, show-offy (except in articles), I chose the second person "you," and "yours." By telling it in terms of "you," the reader can identify; he feels included, your story becomes in essence his or her story, too. Of course they know the author wrote it, but over and over their response was, "That's just the way it is at our house. You're talking about *us!*"

The present tense enabled me to go back and forth in time, using incidents and observations written long before, if I wanted to. Polished up, they were as fresh today as ever; and the technique spared any embarrassment to my children, whom I never referred to by name or age. Substituting, "your little girl," "the oldest," "the teenager," "the four year old," "the baby," or whatever.

Here, in part, are two examples:

"Merry Christmas, Mrs. Scratch!"

"A gingerbread house! Oh, please, let's make a gingerbread house!" the second grader pleads, racing up with a colored picture torn from papers unknown. At your expression: "*Sally's* mother always makes them a gingerbread house every year."

You think frantically of the thousands of more vital things to do — cards, shopping, your own house in a horrendous state. But before this status symbol, you quail, "Well, let's see — if we've got enough gingerbread mix."

"*Mix? Sally's* mother makes everything from scratch."

"They Come In, Cold and Laughing"

They come in, cold and laughing, the other teenage couples who are going to the dance with your daughter and her date. . . . Your husband comes cheerfully up from the basement, where he is making copper gadgets for Christmas. . . . While he's upstairs getting the car keys, one of the girls briskly and inaccurately plays carols, and with blissful lack of harmony, the others sing. . . . Meanwhile, your daughter flashes about doing last minute things — finding a lipstick, fastening some tiny silver bells to her skirt . . . and as you bend near to fasten her pearls, she smells like a rose.

Younger ones, realizing the car is leaving, beg to ride along. And, surprisingly the older ones say "Sure, let 'em, we'll hold 'em." There is an avalanche out the door. . . . And now the house is quiet, but still vibrating with the personalities that have filled it to overflowing. Still warm and bright and lived in, clutter and all.

And standing there in its center, you think — this is it. The best time of life for a woman. And you long to hug it to you, enjoy it to the hilt at this, the very best time of the year.

The Rewards

There is a magic about writing for a newspaper, even if you never go near the place. (I mailed my columns in.) Suddenly — or to be more accurate, gradually — you achieve identity. Your picture appears in the paper regularly (in my case every few days) but far more important, your words. Your audience is almost immediate, and so is its response. Before the day or week is over, you will hear from quite a number of them — and more, as time goes on. I never got over this wonder, which seemed to be happening to somebody else. And no Sunday or Wednesday went by when the *Star* was dropped at our door, that I didn't pick it up with as much anxiety as anticipation; afraid that I might not *be* there (which sometimes happens, when space is tight), or that today's column might not measure up to my expectations.

I think these symptoms are common to a lot of us. But the rewards are worth the price. For one, when you're with a newspaper, doors open, often very important ones, especially in Washington, where celebrities and famous world figures are always making speeches or being entertained. There are dramatic events to attend every day. The old guard take such things for granted, but to an inexperienced columnist they are heady stuff. Not that I took advantage very often; I was too busy raising a family and writing other things — but it was nice to know I *could*. And on the rare occasions when I did go, the experience was always memorable. Particularly, receptions at the White House, which the First Lady gives every year for women of the press.

Books

The column was never syndicated, though some pieces were picked up by other papers, and a few made *Reader's Digest*. There was one prospect with an offer, but the column would have to be daily, and for me that seemed professional suicide. I could have done nothing else, and I had other things to write, particularly books. As it turned out, it was the books that were published because of the column that became the richest reward of all.

After the first few years, Doubleday published a collection called *Love and Laughter*, drawing mainly from my column, but including some of my magazine articles. It did so well they asked for another. Evelyn Metzger, their Washington, D.C. editor, had become my friend through the Press Club. She was also my neighbor, her offices in a small Doubleday building, on the grounds of her beautiful home. We discussed "Apron Pocket Prayers," the category which drew the most mail.

At that time mine seemed to be the only simple, conversational prayers being published, at least for women. Evelyn suggested that if I could accumulate enough (about 100), "They just might make a book." Since I prayed that way anyway, I prayed and wrote harder. Deciding, at the last minute, the day the manuscript was due, to call it *I've Got to Talk to*

Somebody, God. None of us expected much of it; and when the first copy was in my hands, I remember thinking, "Oh, that little *nonbook.*"

To our astonishment, it took off—thanks largely, I'm convinced, to advance publication of ten selections in *Woman's Day*. Suddenly this little "sleeper," was a phenomenal best-seller, with 90,000 copies sold the first three months. As a result, *Woman's Day* signed me to write a monthly column titled, "A Woman's Conversations With God."

Bantam bought paperback rights, not only to the book of prayers, but *Love and Laughter* and my earlier novels. After that, the column spawned books like babies:

As Tall as My Heart and *Beauty in Your Own Backyard*, were bought by EPM, the firm Evelyn formed herself, after leaving Doubleday. *To Treasure Our Days* (Hallmark). Five little books, *A Time for Faith, A Time for Love*, etc. (C.R. Gibson). And at least nine more inspirational books for Doubleday, including, *Hold Me Up a Little Longer, Lord*, (drawn mainly from the *Woman's Day* columns); *Nobody Else Will Listen* (prayers for teenage girls). *Lord, Let Me Love* and *To Help You Through the Hurting* (anthologies of all my writings on the subjects).

And most recently, *At Christmas the Heart Goes Home*, a treasury of the many Christmas articles I wrote for the major magazines, and about fifty holiday columns written for the *Star*.

Every hardback in the above list (and later) was also reprinted in paperback. And all because of a newspaper column which lasted twenty-five years—until I remarried, after the death of my husband, and moved away. Sadly, just as that wonderful old paper, so rich in history, folded.

I miss them both.

I would have written books anyway. During that early period I had written two novels for J.B. Lippincott. Five teenage novels for Westminster Press. And continued with a novel about the birth of Jesus: *Two From Galilee*, which was published, after years of rejection, by Fleming H. Revell. It too became an instant best-seller, and led to a two-part sequel to complete the trilogy: *Three From Galilee—The Young Man From Nazareth*, and *The Messiah*, by Harper & Row. There was also the book of nostalgia, *You and I and Yesterday*, for William Morrow.

But it was my column, with its breakthrough book of prayers, that tipped the first rock of the avalanche.

How a Column Might Help You

I have gone into this at length, in the hope that it might inspire someone else to do likewise. Some truly creative writer who has a fund of charming material, perhaps gathered in notebooks and journals, as mine was. Or even any talented person capable of writing columns from the heart.

You don't have to live in a city; hundreds of men and women have been at it for years in little towns. If there's nothing like it in your area, you're in luck. Prepare some samples and convince your local editor to give you a start. If it catches on, offer it to neighboring newspapers and form your own syndicate.

You don't have to follow my format, although you may want to. If so, you have my blessings. Just invent your own title and categories. If you're truly a talented creative writer, and keep notebooks, you won't have to borrow; you will have more ideas than you can use.

Section 2

Writing Well From the Heart

CHAPTER ELEVEN

The Five Fundamentals

*T*he five fundamentals of a good creative article are:
1. a provocative idea
2. an appropriate style
3. a smooth, sound structure
4. pertinent human anecdotes
5. a good, clear summary or conclusion

A Provocative Idea

The idea, and the way it is presented, is the heart of the creative article — not facts, remember, no matter how wise or well arranged. Just ideas — your own and other people's, about how to make the best of every card life deals us, and win or lose, learn to enjoy the game.

This need is universal. Everybody wants to know.

I can illustrate best by the first question Gene Shalit shot at me on the "Today Show": "Marjorie, why do your books sell so well?"

Instantly, the answer came to me. So fast I wondered why I'd never asked it myself before: "Identification and help," I told him. "If you can write something that makes other people say, 'Hey, that's *me*! how did she know I felt that way?' And at the same time offer them some hope and help for their problems, you will always have an audience."

This goes for everything you write. Especially articles from the heart. The provocative idea is one that makes your story *their* story. They recognize the subject, it's familiar ground, like an old friend with whom the reader feels at home. Reader and writer speak a common language. He trusts you and wants your opinion. He will listen.

Yet another reason he will listen to what you're saying is that this friend is never dull; the writer brings out a bright new slant on things. "Why, I never thought of it that way before," the reader may react. Or vigorously disagree, "No, absolutely not, you're wrong." This is another important secret behind the success of the idea. You, the author, provide insight into an age-old situation; and whether your readers applaud or object, they are never bored. The idea has not only caught people's attention but rewarded them by the fresh, bright way it is developed. Your audience feels both entertained and helped or inspired.

There is, of course, nothing new under the sun. The captivating idea is any idea that makes the old *seem* new. It never belabors the obvious — for instance, "Mothers Should Be Good Examples," or "Happiness Is Important to the Home." Such clichés would only make people shrug, "Of course, so what?" But you can bring to the obvious *an angle of interpretation* that is unique and worth exploring.

I did exactly that several times with exactly those subjects. The first I called, "The Toughest Job of Parenthood," and opened with that statement. Going on to describe how "I entered motherhood sublimely convinced that I would be the perfect parent. I would set such wonderful examples my offspring would all be models of perfection, the darlings of teachers and friends and of course superachievers. . . . Only to discover *nobody's* the perfect parent, and there's no guarantee the kids will turn out likewise even if you were. . . ." The article made the point that setting such goals is not only unrealistic "but it can wear you out and even be destructive, turning Mom into a martyr or a martinet and making everybody miserable."

The very same theme (parental perfection) triggered another piece, by simply changing the angle of interpretation. This time light humor: "Please Don't Name Me Mother of the Year!" A partly true story of the time the family wrote a skit kidding Mom's foibles in her frantic attempts to teach Sunday School as well as be den mother and president of PTA.

The second subject (homes should be happy), was saved from a didactic obviousness by a straightforward approach: "How to Keep Home Life Happy." In this article I accepted the obvious. Okay, so sweet harmony in your home is important, now what do we do to achieve it? Using anecdotes and examples of schemes that worked for us and for other families, I hit the subject head-on and offered a list of *specific suggestions*. Thus the piece sang right along and sounded fresh.

Sometimes ideas will come that seem way-out to you, intriguing because they are actually so farfetched. Don't be too quick to dismiss them. Use the "what-if" technique so common to fiction writers. What if you had acted on that impulse to jump on a fire truck and join the action? Could you have saved somebody? What if you actually left your important job to go to that school for clowns? Volunteer for a dangerous spy mission, become a government witness, run for President, give some poor kid your entire month's salary? What effect would it have on your life, the city, mankind, your marriage? What message, serious or light would it bring? We are all at times Mr. and Mrs. Mittys, and what appears fantastic is often an echo of everybody's secret dreams.

Sometimes excellent personal experience stories are born out of such ideas, when the writer has the courage to act them out.

Never strain for the unusual, however — the strain will show. The best ideas are generally those that emerge from the simple everyday stuff of our own existence. Yours, mine, the people next door. The more you write the more you will be able to recognize that quality of something special, something unique that shines from the ordinary, and makes you cry out, "Hey, that's it. That's a good idea!"

An Appropriate Style

What makes the article from the heart successful is not only the idea, but *the way it is written*. This means both structure and style. For now, let's consider just two aspects of the style: It must be clear and readable, never dryly pedantic or obscure. And it must be *appropriate* both to the subject matter and to the author's interpretation.

It should be apparent that articles from the heart must sound warm, and even in controversy, sincere. And a light, humorous touch is like music and sunshine wherever it fits the occasion. But there are some subjects where it would be fatal to be funny. Death, for instance — except for rare occasions.

I once saw a student manuscript called "Great Aunt Annie's Funeral." Now, had the author's *approach* been even moderately respectful, a mild sort of humor could have tastefully emerged from the gathering of a warring clan at the bier of an eccentric. Instead, the approach was slapstick, one long sick joke at the expense of a good woman and grieving people. I suppose this sort of thing could be done for, say, a funeral director's journal ("A Funny Thing Happened on the Way to the Funeral," maybe), but for general readership a flip style about a serious matter like death is unacceptable.

Likewise, a light or humorous tone or style would have been woefully inappropriate for another article I wrote for *Better Homes and Gardens* — "Protect Your Child From Sex Offenders." It opened with an anecdote — our little girl's skipping around the corner to play with a neighbor's children, and her obedient phone call home less than five minutes later when she arrived. It proceeded to tell why these and other precautions were taken — all in a conversational style, not grim, but certainly never amusing. The subject of children's safety is treated over and over in current magazine articles. Note the style and tone used for such serious issues. And how the style changes for subjects less critical: getting along with a roommate, for instance, or sharing housework. Such everyday things can be treated either lightly or more seriously, depending on your feeling for the material and the point you want to make. Just be sure your style and tone are appropriate, not only for the subject but for the magazine you are aiming for.

Articles of protest or controversy call for their own sprightly, brisk, sometimes brittle, sometimes funny, but always forceful, straightforward style. On the other hand, essays of reminiscence require a flowing and lyrical style in keeping with the emotions you are trying to express.

As you read, note how writers adapt their style to their material.

A Smooth, Sound Structure

The basic idea which launches the article and permeates it must be made very clear by discussion, and illustrated, usually by anecdote. The manner in which this material is organized is its structure or form. The well-written article, like the well-written short story, reads so easily and smoothly that it is often difficult to realize that the form is there.

Sometimes we do find articles from the heart which seem to ramble and backtrack unnecessarily, yet make their point and make it well. Okay, fine. The idea may itself be so vital, the writing style so impressive that the structure can pretty much go hang; it will still come out all right. Enjoy these pieces, but don't be misled by them. Most creative articles follow certain patterns of organization (as you will be shown), not because anybody made a rule about it, but simply because they are more effective that way.

Pertinent Human Anecdotes

Anecdotes are simply little stories that demonstrate the writer's point and make his message clear.

The idea is the heart or soul of the article.

The structure is its skeleton or body.

Its style may be considered its personality.

But it is the anecdotes which activate every article from the heart and make it live!

If you are writing the personal experience article you may want to use only one major illustration or story. But this primary event or situation is usually led up to, fortified and interpreted by several lesser episodes or incidents which contribute to the story.

The Inspirational Sketch is another type in which a single anecdote, often seemingly slight, may be given total focus. In most articles, however, particularly those of advice or discussion, a number of anecdotes are used. Seldom fewer than three or more than six. I have counted as many as nine sometimes, in scanning magazine pieces, but four or five are an average for articles running from 1,500 to 2,500 words.

"Where do you get your anecdotes?" is a question asked almost as often as "Where do you get your ideas?" Just as I've said about ideas, you get them from life itself. From friends, relatives, neighbors; those people you meet or overhear on buses or in theater lobbies, or wherever you are. From people very much like your readers, with whom readers can identify. Each one with stories to tell, similarly from the heart. Use them. A writer should realize that other people's stories can inspire and embellish your own. The end result will be writing that reaches into even more lives and hearts.

What do people discuss at family reunions or coffee-klatsches? People! Mainly to express their own views about a situation. Listen, and learn:

"She's gone back to work, and Bill's upset. He wants her to stay home and look after the baby, and I don't blame him. When people wait as long as they have for a child, you'd think she'd want to take care of it herself . . . especially when you hear what's going on in day care centers these days."

"No, I don't think she's going to do that. I hear the grandmother's coming to look after it. What a mistake! I'd never have an in-law living in my house again. I tried it —"

"Oh, I don't know. Jack's mother lives with us, and we get along beautifully. To tell you the truth, I don't know how we'd get along without her."

Thus out of the anecdote about one person spring anecdotes from the experiences of others, and all to prove or disprove an attitude or conviction.

Or children bring you their tales from camp and club and school — stories wacky and wild and wonderful, pertinent or pathetic; some so revealing of human truth that you hasten to your notebook to set them down. Many are simply absorbed, deposited without your actually knowing it into your memory bank, from which one day, suddenly, you will make a quick and apt withdrawal.

Frequently the anecdotes must be built up or toned down, altered to suit our purpose; or we invent others that will. This is just as legitimate in the creative article as it is in fiction, where the author's finest characters are composites of many people. The ultimate result seems and sounds even more true because the author has trained the sharp lens of his camera upon some basic essential common to most people.

It is sometimes better to invent people and incidents anyway, so they can't recognize themselves. Don't use your boss or your next-door neighbor to illustrate negative characteristics — at least not until you've moved far away, and even then it's best to use "disguises." Naturally you'd never use anyone's real name or even initials, with these exceptions: articles of family reminiscence where the reference is complimentary; or anecdotes of famous people.

Warm human tales from the lives of famous people, past or present, can be a boon to your articles. They add flavor and substance to your theme. But don't make the mistake of using stock anecdotes about historical figures like Ben Franklin and his kite, Washington and the cherry tree, or Lincoln walking miles to return a penny.

If you do use eminent names to enhance and enliven your illustration, be on the lookout for little known facts about them in biographies or gossip columns, interviews and speeches. Their stories are especially moving if told by the celebrity himself. Few people were born rich and famous. Most of them had to struggle, just as we do. And the fact that even the stars of stage and screen and sports and even former presidents have, like us, had their doubts and failures, draws us all together as members of the human family, reaching out as best we can to inspire and encourage and help each other.

This is not research, in the usual sense. For me, it's fun.

Keep in mind that anecdotes should be fresh, never clichés; and they should reveal universal truths or highlight the point you want to make.

How do writers identify the principals in anecdotes? Sometimes by inventing names, as you would in writing fiction — Jerry Faversham, Mrs. Johnson, Father O'Boyle. (In writing humor, you can achieve some wonderfully funny effects with names.) Or you can simply fall back on "My friend Jane." Names like "Jane B." or "Oscar R." are in disfavor — they smack somehow of the coy or phony. Perhaps the best device is simply to identify by occupation, profession or group: "A college professor told me — ," "A young married woman down the street — ," "Our daughter's English teacher — ," "A pretty girl just back from the Peace Corps — ."

Showing the kind of people they are and what they do serves the double purpose of making their observations more valid in the context of the anecdote. Remember: anecdotes are used for a purpose. Quote freely; let *them* tell their stories. In the interest of brevity, simply condense their experiences: "I knew a brilliant woman lawyer who had put four children through college — 'without ever really knowing them' she told me. 'I was always in court or consulting with a client, when often they needed to consult me even more desperately.' "

Dialogue is important in writing an anecdote. And, as in fiction, it should do these things: Characterize, advance the movement, give the reader information. In the creative article, it must do one thing more: *Prove the point.* A sentence, even a fragment of conversation, is often the capsule of the message: "I wish I knew my children better — ," "Don't be afraid to be friendly," "Grandpa always said — 'everybody's really kin-folk — ,' " " 'Don't wait too long to go after what you want,' the professor warned." " 'The meek don't inherit the earth,' Dad said to Peter when he was going off to take his first job in Los Angeles."

Whatever the article type, the dialogue should be succinct and telling. It should be used in the anecdote for a definite purpose: to characterize the individual and underscore the circumstances which are being used to illustrate the theme.

A Good, Clear Summary or Conclusion

Some articles just stop, leaving the reader to draw his own conclusions; articles can be very effective that way. Most articles, however, summarize what has been said. A good article should: "Tell 'em what you're going to tell 'em. Tell 'em. Then tell 'em what you've told 'em."

This "tell 'em what you've told 'em" is the packaging of the theme. In the advice article, a good way to do this is to cite and clarify the various points you have made under rules or suggestions, listed numerically: For instance: 1. Decide what you most want to do in life. 2. Train for it. 3. Go where the opportunities are.

The final point can be your final statement. Or you can go a step further and "tie a bow on the package," by making one last conclusive statement, shining and memorable, you hope. This is just one of those extras that help an article to sell.

CHAPTER TWELVE

Tone, Focus and Pace

*T*here is a subtle but real relationship between tone and style. Actually, the tone of an article is in part created by the style in which it is written. But there is another very important aspect of tone which comes from the author's own emotions and point of view. Its *sound* must come from the heart.

Two equally fine symphony orchestras composed of the same instruments may play the same composition, but the music will sound very different — first, because of their particular styles and second, because of their special tones.

The writer, as conductor, is using words with all the skill at his command. He may be a humorist who writes a clever piece, yet it fails because it sounds smug, unkind, contemptuous. Or the writer may be a woman describing how she coped with sorrow. Her story may be valid and essentially moving; she may have organized it well; the writing may be smooth. Yet again it may fall flat because it is depressing or smacks of self-pity, or contrarily be even too glib in its resolution. If so, the whole thing *sounds* wrong, she has simply hit upon the wrong *tone*.

Generally speaking, articles from the heart should be pleasantly conversational in tone. Advice articles definitely should be so, otherwise their tone will become bossy, preachy, didactic. Articles with the light touch, straight humor or otherwise, should never sound coy, self-conscious or cute. Their tone should be merry without being flippant. Articles of inspirational quality should sound gentle, even tender, but never sentimental or sticky sweet. Articles of controversy or protest should sound forceful and even angry in places, but never caustic, sarcastic or too grim. Otherwise, they become diatribe, their storm and fury repelling the reader instead of interesting and arousing him. Articles of personal experience should neither smack of "poor me," nor swagger and boast. Another tone that sometimes slips into such articles is one of amazement: how exciting it all was, how frightened we were, how relieved at last. And it should be self-evident that any thoughtful article on any serious subject should never slip into coyness or flippancy or any other sins which jar the general tone.

There should be a prevailing mood or tone, deriving from four elements: the author's *style*; his *attitude* toward his material; the *point of view* from which the author writes the article; and the *basic premise* or point he is trying to make.

All or several of these elements are, surprisingly, lacking in many amateur's attempts at creative articles. Unsure of their own viewpoints, confused in their attitudes, never quite able to pin down the actual premise, the authors of such articles write too much about too little, and achieve no satisfactory overall tone.

It will be helpful, I hope, to examine the factors which can produce the wrong tone.

Wrong Subject

True, anything in the world can be written about humorously or gently or constructively if the treatment results in the appropriate tone. But some subjects are better avoided, unless you are careful — minority groups, for instance; classes of people, especially the service classes (truck and cabdrivers, waitresses, hairdressers, maids, etc.); the handicapped and the underprivileged.

In articles from the heart, of course, we are not dealing with classes or particular conditions of people per se. We are dealing with human behavior, with emotions, with philosophy. But if any one kind or class of people provides your major illustration, you must bring a special measure of understanding to the task.

To illustrate: I have before me a student manuscript which is supposed to be funny, and could be. The writing itself is deft, the wisecracks witty. The subject, however, is borderline: a wife's running battle with waitresses — a subject that could be hilarious, if skillfully handled, or become downright embarrassing and unkind.

The opening is brisk:

Tonight I look forward to having a good dinner after my wife's fight. If I've given the impression that my wife is a woman wrestler, I should explain. I'm referring to her fight with waitresses in any restaurant to which I take her. From the first moment she and a waitress lock eyes, there is a sensed hostility, as if they were but renewing old wars waged on distant battlefields of long ago. . . . It goes like this—

He orders a table for two, and assures the reader that his wife is a very sweet person under any other circumstance. But now the inevitable is about to begin. By the third paragraph, I, along with the husband, was beginning to feel embarrassed. By the fourth I was squirming before the wife's unreasoning rudeness. By the fifth I wanted to smack her for being so nasty to ''Big Bertha,'' the outsized, slow-moving waitress. And when the wife sent back her steak and she and her husband left, laughing gaily at the waitress' consternation, I was filled with sad dismay. No amount of clever writing can compensate for cruelty. What might have been an amusing satire about a wife's peccadillo, simply makes fun of a less fortunate human being. The tone of the entire piece is ridicule.

Earlier I gave as a bad example the slapstick treatment of a funeral. Any article dealing with any aspect of death must be done very perceptively and sensitively indeed to strike a tone that will not offend. Or, almost as bad, get overemotional. After class one day a beautiful woman came to me with tears in her eyes, beseeching me to criticize an account she had written of her little girl's fatal accident. I accepted it with apprehension, praying that it would be well done—since I shrank from adding further to her hurt. But tragedy is very hard to discuss, especially if its wounds are recent. The grief-stricken tone plunged the piece into melodrama. Such outpourings are not articles; they are soul purges that are better left in the desk drawer. I told her to put her article away and not even try to write of this experience until she could bring some detachment to it. I advised her to write on other subjects.

In skilled hands, such tragedies can be moving and inspiring to others. But the unseasoned writer would do well to choose other topics.

As for physical afflictions—your long bout with illness, your operation—there *is* a tremendous reader interest in health and the human body, in how to overcome the enemies that beset it. But so many people deluge editors with badly written blow-by-blow descriptions, written in the tone of "let me tell about my operation!" that your treatment in the article must be exceptional to merit consideration.

Well, what about sex? Now *there's* a surefire subject. Or is it? Don't be seduced by all that sex you see on magazine covers. Writing about sex and achieving just the right tone is a very difficult thing to do. Unless your attitudes are very sound and your writing very good, leave sex to the sexperts.

Wrong Attitude

A perfectly safe subject such as home, children, friends, can be ruined by an attitude of condescension, superiority and egotism on the author's part. If you bring any of these attitudes to your material, no matter how good your writing, how fine your organization, or how cogent your arguments, that attitude will permeate and subtly poison the entire piece.

I have been guilty of this on several occasions. Years ago, provoked by a certain person who continually freeloaded, borrowed without returning, and was a born brain-picker, I wrote an article deploring such traits. So as not to offend the original model, I parceled these traits out among a number of hypothetical, obnoxious characters. The whole thing stood up technically, but my attitude of utter annoyance and chagrin over something I was too weak to correct, wrecked the tone. It was not pleasant reading.

I have had to revise articles about raising children. "Forgive me but you sound a little superior," one editor wrote. A rereading proved her right—I certainly did. I had *felt* superior in relating the wise and wonderful methods we were using in raising our children, as contrasted to the mistakes some other parents were making. (Such egotism is less of a hazard as you grow older. In fact, you're less prone to preach to parents about anything!)

Preaching is another tone that results from self-righteousness. "We buy articles, not sermons," an editor once scribbled across the face of one of my early efforts. I was angry and hurt—but she was actually doing me a favor. I remembered to stay out of the pulpit, to speak with humility as well as conviction in the articles I wrote therafter.

Self-pity is an attitude to guard against, as well. Feeling lonely and unloved, or overwhelmed by the sheer unfairness of it all, we are sometimes inspired to sit down and write away our miseries. This can be excellent therapy, but it does not make for interesting articles. Other people are so busy feeling sorry for themselves they don't want to be bothered feeling sorry for you. If they are to share your wretchedness in any constructive way, it will be because your *attitude* states clearly, "Look, I know I'm not the only one. I tackled this problem or this situation in this way and came out better for it. So can you." But again your attitude cannot be, "how brave I am." I once worked on a manuscript for a woman who devoted years to finding help for a mentally disturbed child. Her experiences were dramatic, and she showed real courage and gallantry. But repeatedly I had to warn, "Don't sound so sorry for yourself." Or, "Don't pose. You're just too self-consciously brave here."

Not all negative attitudes are wrong. Indignation, impatience, outrage — all can be effective occasionally. They can even be converted into something amusing. For a while I tapped a lucrative vein that came straight out of an attitude of distress: "Guests I Detest," "Hostesses I Abhor," "How to Lose Your Mailman," "How to Punish the Plumber." But the attitude of female fury and flurry succeeded because it was not meant to belittle or hurt anyone; it was simply good-humored satire of everybody's foibles, and the *tone* of good humor kept it fun.

You will find examples of friendly but funny annoyances in almost every magazine that uses humor, and from the syndicated columnists to items in your local paper. Read them to observe and perhaps absorb their special tone.

If the writer is seriously concerned about something, however, his attitude should show it. "Get mad!" an editor once urged in asking me to revise a piece of mild protest. "Let 'em have it." In this instance, my attitude was wrong primarily because I wasn't sufficiently incensed. And if I weren't personally aroused, why should anyone else be?

Currently, I *am* mad at what seems to me the invasion of *my* privacy by having the sex lives of total strangers thrust upon me. Fed up, I queried

Reader's Digest about "A Plea for Old-Fashioned Privacy," which they assigned and bought. It was also published in *The PTA Magazine*, where it was spotted by a child psychologist and used in a court case concerning the damage such material can do to children.

Write while the adrenaline is still surging. Furious at the flagrant anti-Americanism of some of Yevtushenko's poems read at his New York concert, I flew home from Madison Square Garden to compose "An Open Letter to Yevtushenko," where I challenged him to accord me the same freedom and facilities to attack Communism in the Kremlin. The letters that poured in from that one — mostly from refugees and Soviet victims — again proved that these articles of passionate protest or exhortation can have far-reaching effects.

No Point of View

If you have no clear point of view, you can make no point. Thus you will have produced an article that really has nothing to say, and so cannot achieve the quality of total tone.

As I said initially, the author of articles from the heart approaches problems with both logic and emotion. He cannot hurl himself sobbing into the article (as in the example of the bereaved mother) or he will lose all sense of logic, and with it his *point of view*. Neither can he remain detached from his material. Logic alone will then prevail, minus any emotional involvement; he will have lost that passion, that conviction, that again results in *point of view*.

This may seem like a complicated way of stating a very simple point. But think about it a minute, and I believe you'll agree. You must have not only one definite, desirable *attitude* toward your subject; you must also be very clear about where you stand on it. To determine this, first ask: What is this article all about? When you have established that, you can proceed to turn out a work which says something, holds together and achieves the right tone. When you do not — when you bring in too many subjects, cover too much material, explore too many emotions, display diverse attitudes — the article winds up a hodgepodge, lacking any single tone, or worse, so out of focus that the theme cannot come through.

Focus

Focus is very important to an article. This means simply that the picture it portrays is clear instead of fuzzy and diffuse. A photographer has to train his camera on a subject and adjust his lens so that the result will be sharp and unmistakable — in short, in focus. The writer must do exactly the same thing. Newspaper writers call the central point of any story, their "angle." I have referred to it earlier as your "angle of interpretation." When we speak of focus, we mean simply concentrating upon that angle.

The writer must decide what his subject actually is. And then bring to it only material that will contribute to the final, unmistakable effect. Every sentence must somehow achieve this purpose or it is extraneous and must be ruthlessly cut out.

"But this will make my article read like an outline!" protested one student who had written 3,000 words that so fogged and clouded what I presumed was her original image that I proposed cutting the article in half. She herself was not sure just what her article was trying to say. By discarding half of what she had written and sternly focusing all the rest on one specific phase, or angle, of her discussion, there was a chance of saving it. Actually, however, the entire 3,000 words might have had a legitimate excuse for being there had they been so arranged and directed that they *emphasized her point,* rather than diverted the reader from it.

Before you can learn to focus, you must decide: What is this article all about? What is its basic message or theme?

Here are some examples:

The manuscript just referred to began promisingly: An opening anecdote in which the author described her first reactions to the loss of her husband. The sense of loneliness, of being at loose ends, of trying to find some reason for going on. . . . Yes, yes, *do* go on — but not much further! I began to react. Get to the point. How did you solve this important and common problem? What do you propose?

Well, first she visited her sister in Boston, and then she remembered her childhood days in Texas, and next she seemed to be on a boat to Europe with a description of fellow passengers. Then she was in Athens, where the taxidrivers must be watched, and the food is good at a little place just off Syntagma Square, and from her windows she could look down on the old Royal Palace, now the home of the Greek Parliament, and after a few days exploring the ruins there —

What emerged from many pages was neither advice nor philosophy, neither personal adventure nor travelogue. The article was long, wordy and totally disorganized, mainly because it had no focus. It had no overriding purpose or ultimate message. It said a lot about too many things, and in the end had nothing to say.

Or take a manuscript by another student, in a lighter vein: The title was so delightful she may still be able to use it, so I won't give it away here. A rough and very inferior paraphrase: "You Kids Lay Off My Piano." Written by a piano teacher, it started out describing the havoc pupils can wreak on the instructor's instrument. They bang it, they kick it, they often scratch it with pencils, rulers or their fingernails. So far, so good. The article could have been amusing, exploring this hazard further. Or it could have led into a light but firm discussion as to how to train the little demons to avert the damage — to both instrument and teacher's temper.

There were two excellent possibilities, in fact, either one of which could have been briskly and engagingly followed. But, no. We were presently learning about music conservatories, their cost, merits and locations. And about the author's childhood, and how hard she had to practice. Then came something about her romance with a tall, handsome harpist, and how he didn't want her to give piano lessons; and about her mother's old piano, which had a much better sounding board than those you get, especially in spinets, today.

As the words piled up, I began to count, in a kind of fascination, the angles on which she might have focused to draw a good article out of this loosely thrown together batch of material, and bemoaned the fact that if she had only decided *which one* she was going to emphasize, she could have made the other incidents, disparate though they were, related to that central objective. Each little tale or argument could have been trimmed and shaped to fit neatly into the framework of her composition.

Or, again, she might have focused on the career of a piano teacher: Her own childhood experiences leading up to this hour; the opposition of her husband; her ultimate trials and triumphs. It might have focused on pianos themselves, her mother's sturdy instrument vs. those today; how to choose one that can stand up under the onslaught of bratty kids.

By deciding on her angle and bringing it into focus, she might have used every incident to lighten, shade, enhance or clarify her central subject. It would have had some reason for being there. Instead, we had a batch of mildly interesting ideas going in their different directions, resulting only in confusion and fuzziness.

Cures

Here are a few suggestions to cure this confusion and restore focus:

1. Cut everything that does not bear directly upon your point. In the case of the bereaved widow, this would eliminate lengthy descriptions of problems with customs agents and people encountered on the ship, for instance.

2. If you feel that some section has an obscure bearing on your point and you want to keep it, *refocus*, reshape and reslant that particular material so that it does relate directly to your central theme.

To illustrate, even a hassle with customs agents *could* be made to bear upon the problems of a widow traveling alone for the first time. ("The whole world may seem to be against her at first — this stranger pawing through the luggage. . . .") Or encounters on shipboard could be turned into anecdotes that helped to prove or disprove something. (People's solicitude, or their indifference. Discovering others with a similar problem, how sharing helps, advice received, etc.)

But unless something serves to sharpen up the angle, or make your theme more significant, it has no business there.

3. Put a figure of speech to work. In one of my articles about marriage problems I used an old but strong analogy, the sea of matrimony. "No matter how romantically you set off, it won't be a cruise on the Love Boat. There are bound to be rocks and shoals and sometimes stormy waters ahead. . . ."

I continue to use the metaphor to draw together, sharpen and keep in focus several elements that might have gone wandering off and become ineffectual: quarrels about work, money, other couples, children, in-laws, sex. The possibilities of divorce or separation. Keeping all this firmly cohesive and clear by using such phrases as, "From minor squals to hurricanes," "It takes two to row a boat," "Don't be too quick to abandon ship."

Though the article covers a lot of water, the reader isn't futilely trying to swim to some undefined shore. The piece itself reaches safe harbor because the reader knows exactly where the author has taken him.

Pace

If you keep your point clearly in focus, you are far more likely to achieve that precious sense of timing known as pace. Pace is absolutely essential to any form of writing.

Pace is movement. Pace is a sense of forward motion that is always smooth and rhythmic as it leads — or carries — the reader swiftly toward the goal.

An appropriate analogy is horse racing. As youngsters we used to watch the harness races at the county fair. When the gun went off, the horses sprang forward, pulling their little carts behind them. Then, very often as the crowd cheered a favorite rounding a far corner, a mass groan would go up: "Oh, he broke, he's lost his pace!" That is the original term, and no doubt where writers actually got it. And how accurate it is! Just as a horse who loses his stride in any way cannot hope to finish a winner, neither can an article or short story. It too must surge swiftly ahead, pounding out its smooth, inevitable rhythms. It cannot jump fences to explore neighboring pastures, go back to the gate to start over, pause to nibble grass, shy at bright objects, or balk. It must run confidently forward.

Then stop.

Pace is partly a matter of style, a delicate balancing of the phrases that carry the writer's thoughts. As you progress as a writer, you begin to develop a sixth sense of timing or pace. Even when you use the flashback technique (cutting back in sequence of events to supply information), that sense of forward motion is still there. Since the seeming interruption, the flashback, occurs for the purpose of leading right back to the present and beyond it, the subtle, steady beat of pace continues to be felt.

The more you write, the more skilled you will become at controlling that vital element, pace.

The tone. The focus. The pace. Observe them as you read. Make them a part of your inner awareness. Elusive as they are, they are important; mark them in the margins of your consciousness.

CHAPTER THIRTEEN

Three Surefire Ways to Organize What You Have to Say

*T*he best way to make a dress or to build a boat or a house is to follow a pattern or blueprint. And very few cooks can imagine working without recipes. True, creative people can and do fashion their own patterns and recipes all the time, or they take tested ones and bring variations to them.

Similarly, in writing, certain formulas are used (despite a lot of breast-beating and saying oh, no, we shouldn't) simply because they have proved effective. Madeleine L'Engle expressed it well "Neither you nor I can teach anybody to write. We can, however, point out that in all great writing there are certain things the masters always do, and there are certain things they never do, and we can learn from these."

The anecdote-and-discussion form of creative article is probably the most *natural* form of human discourse; it is also one of the most ancient. The Bible is filled with examples of truth vividly demonstrated through incidents in the lives of people. The effective use of this form is particularly apparent in the New Testament, where we find Jesus teaching and preaching in parables. He would first state his premise and then prove its validity by means of a story to which his listeners could relate. And he drew the substance of these parables from the common fund of their experience — fishing, farming, paying taxes. All his analogies and even most of his metaphors were easily recognizable to his listeners, yet succinct and often startling.

In our own experiences today, it is almost impossible to have any exchange of ideas about human relationships without following a similar form. Listen to almost any discussion about almost any subject of common interest: "I don't believe in co-ed dorms in college, and I'll tell you why. My daughter (or neighbor, son, or nephew) went through it—" And a little story is told to illustrate the speaker's convictions.

Meanwhile, the other person is waiting to chime in with his or her comments: "You're right. Kids are too young to handle it. My sister couldn't study, she had to move out—" Or perhaps, "Why, I lived in a co-ed dorm and thought it was great! I'd never had a brother, it was wonderful having boys around as well as girls—I learned a lot from them."

As I mentioned earlier, such conversations often provide the writer with usable anecdotes. Here, I want simply to point out that conversation follows an uncontrived, almost inevitable form. The progression is logical and natural. Perhaps that is why the intuitive or natural writer, or the experienced one, so often uses dialogue without even thinking about it. But the novice, not yet attuned to the fact that all writing should emerge and fall *naturally* into its most logical form, freezes up before his material. He struggles to "write an article," self-consciously putting in everything he can think of about his subject in an unnatural and literary manner. The result is often pedantic, chaotic or both.

This, of course, is not to say that the article from the heart is composed of scraps of dialogue. It simply follows a similar basic framework.

Here are two of these patterns, plus suggestions for a third:

Pattern One

1. The opening: Begin with straight statement of your theme, followed by an illustrative anecdote or two

Or

   Begin with one or two illustrative anecdotes followed by a statement of your theme.
2. Anticipate the opposition. (This can be done in the very opening, or later in the article.)
3. Enlarge upon the first anecdote, and/or
4. Use other anecdotes that further illustrate your theme.
5. Link illustrations together by discussion of this theme.

6. In an article of advice, real or implied, conclude with specific suggestions, sometimes enumerated.
7. Summarize with a final statement or paragraph which re-emphasizes the theme.

Pattern Two

1. The opening: Start out with a few paragraphs which discuss your theme, or start with one good anecdote.
2. Anticipate your opposition.
3. Lead into specific points or suggestions: 1. 2. 3., enlarging upon each one as you go, and:
4. Use anecdotes and/or discuss each as you proceed.
5. Summarize briefly, or simply stop.

Pattern Three (Your Own)

If you have sufficient imagination, originality, a sense of pace and logic, you can wander as far from these two suggested frameworks as you please. You can invent or use other forms: the letter, the diary, the dream, the dialogue. Or you can present the material in your own way, cutting out anything that is extraneous; a readable though unstructured form quite likely will evolve.

Patterns One and Two apply primarily to the article of advice or of controversy. By analyzing such articles in the magazines, you will quickly see how continually these two formulas are used.

Pattern Three applies mostly to articles of reminiscence, personal experience, humor, or the short inspirational essay. These are categories for which there are no dependable formulas, since they depend so much upon style and tone.

Openings

The opening is one of the most important elements in the article, because it must capture the reader's interest. Here are some examples of the straight *statement* opening:

"Marriage was meant to be enjoyed. Yet the carefree side of marriage is often one of the first fond dreams to go by the board." (One of my articles in *Better Homes and Gardens*.)

Others I have used for various magazines: "Don't be too good a sport. If you're always too cheerful about losing, you may be courting failure." "One of the most important lessons in life that we can learn and ought to teach our children is: Do the thing you dread. And do it *now*."

These openings tackle the subject head on. They inform the reader what this article is going to be all about. The sentences are reasonably short, and there is a certainty even in the rhythms. In each instance the theme is fleshed out with a few more sentences to give it body and substance. Then follows the first proof by means of an illustrative anecdote.

In the marriage article:

One of the most congenial pairs of our acquaintance were the Vales. Together they had built a summer cottage, even built their own swimming pool where friends flocked. Winters they entertained every other Saturday night, and on alternate ones went out. Yet, Mrs. Vale told me, the first ten years of their marriage, they had almost no friends, no fun. [Note contrast.]

In "Do the Thing You Dread":

For weeks a teenage son had stewed himself almost into nervous prostration, so great was his dread of asking a certain girl to the senior prom. When at last the deed was done, he turned from the telephone limp but elated. "Why, she actually sounded thrilled. I bet I could have been dating her all this time! Gee, if I'd only had the nerve sooner — "

I refrained from saying, "I told you so." My own experiences in the living-with-dread department have been too frequent. But I have finally come to grips with the realization: To keep putting anything off, whether a serious ordeal or something merely disagreeable, is to prolong and multiply its misery. Whereas *doing* it is seldom half as bad as we imagined.

Now any of these articles *could* have opened just as well with the anecdote (or other dramatic proof) itself. Reread them as if they were article openings, and you will see how easily they could have been so transposed. My decision to state my thesis and discuss it a bit first was merely a matter of my own feeling toward the material. It simply came out better for me that way.

Putting the anecdote first, however, is very much in favor. It makes the article open like a little story. It hooks the reader's interest because it deals with people. Once he is intrigued by this example or quotation from life, he is ready for the basic idea. He will listen while the author enlarges that idea, emphasizes it and illustrates it further.

Here are some examples of anecdotal openings, which are followed by their themes.

I began "It Takes a Little Nerve" like this:

> As a child, my mother never particularly cared to have us play with Judy because, she said, "She's got such a lot of nerve. . . ."

The theme, immediately following that opening anecdote: "I've come to believe since, however, that a dash of Judy's nerve would have been good for the shyly squelched rest of us; that often fools who rush in where angels fear to flutter *get places angels don't and have a better time.*"

Another of my articles, which appeared as "How Much Sentiment at Your House?" in *Ladies' Home Journal*, began:

> "Oh, but he's just a baby," a friend blithely dismissed our little guy's birthday, in urging us to attend a party the other day, "he won't know the difference if you're not there."
>
> "No, but I will," I said, "and so will the other children. He's got to have a candle and a cake and pictures to prove it, even if he is only a year old. *Because we believe in sentiment for children.* We consider it as important to them as spinach or Sunday School." [Note specifics.]

Anticipate the Opposition

Quite obviously articles of protest would not be written if a lot of people didn't already believe otherwise. And it's hard to conceive of any opinion worthy of any discussion that would not have its exceptions, and its dissenters. Some writers may not even mention this; some may leave it until the end of the article. But I think it is an important and most effective technique (it adds that extra, *contrast*) to acknowledge the exception or the opposition at the outset — and then knock it down as soon as possible.

Sometimes an author opens with a statement of the opposing view, intending to disprove it. In my article "Do You Dare to Be Honest in Marriage?", the title is the opening question, answered by:

> Now let the record be clear to start. Marriage should be based on truth. Any two people heading for the altar are also headed for trouble unless they've been honest about things that count . . . [specifically cited].
>
> But beyond this firm foundation there is a wide area where it is both personally expedient and often downright wholesome, to touch up or trim down the truth.

Before you challenge this with arguments, *concede* certain points.

Returning now to Pattern One: Having taken care of the opposition, enlarge upon the first anecdote or introduce others to illustrate your point. You can, of course, do both. Meanwhile, continue to discuss and prove that point or theme. In other words, link these illustrations through your own comments. Then conclude with some definite suggestions.

A study of published articles will reveal how consistently this particular pattern, with its list of final rules or suggestions, is followed.

Pattern Two is simply a variation of Pattern One: Open with either one good anecdote or a discussion of your theme. Then, instead of putting the specific suggestions at the end, build the entire body of your article upon them. For anyone who has trouble with organization, this is an excellent device. Time and again, struggling with material that somehow would not fall smoothly into place, I have started over, using the 1. 2. 3. method, and had the article surge successfully forward. It is also a form the reader finds easy to follow.

To illustrate, let's analyze an article written on request for *Family Circle*, "Goodbye, Family — Hello, World!", about the woman who has chosen to stay home and raise her children, instead of pursuing a career or job of her own, and what to do when the job of Motherhood is almost over.

> Mrs. Jackson swept the last grains of rice from the rug, carried the final box of tissue paper to the attic, and sat down on the steps to face a fact long postponed: Daughter Jean was married now; son David a senior in college. While Bill, just graduating from high school, had joined the Coast Guard.
>
> "Why, I'm *through!*" thought Mrs. Jackson. "My husband has twenty years still with his company—I haven't any more years with mine. I'm about to retire!"

This is followed by five paragraphs contrasting the plight of such women, who may or may not be eager to rush into the job market, where there is so much competition, especially after so long. How will Mrs. Jackson spend the rest of her life? the article asks. And how can each younger Mrs. Jackson prepare now for that inevitable time?

The article then presents six definite items of advice, each followed by two or three paragraphs of discussion and anecdote pertinent to that suggestion.

1. She can give her "retirement" thoughtful attention while her flock is still around. . . .
2. She can study, grow, develop her special talents and practice them now in many ways. . . .
3. She can guard against becoming too wrapped up in her family. . . .

My article then surveys the vast field of public service and cites definite places where women are not only finding rich rewards, but careers in helping the rest of the world go round.

The conclusion then wraps the whole thing up by reverting right back to the opening, which if possible, is always the most effective way to end:

> There is no reason for any Mrs. Jackson to dread her time of retirement. No excuse for self-pity, for squandering the precious years that can mean so much in self-discovery and the thrill of the outgoing heart. Certainly not if she starts preparing now.
>
> If she does, she won't be sitting on the bottom step for long.

She'll realize with a sense of adventure: "Goodbye, Family—Hello, World!"

As I have said, you needn't be bound by these patterns. You may be sufficiently ingenious to create your own from time to time. But if you write very many creative articles, you'll find yourself following one of these patterns, often without even planning to, because they're so natural a method of persuasive expression. And if you do have a good idea and don't know quite how to present it, try Pattern One or Two. Like our hypothetical heroine, you won't sit staring into space (or at your typewriter) for long.

CHAPTER FOURTEEN

Six Ways to Make Your Articles Better

*T*here are several tools that contribute to the success of articles from the heart. Keep them in mind; they can improve your work and help you reach more people. They are: contrast and comparison, color, characterization, timeliness, specifics and memory devices.

Contrast and Comparison

Contrast and comparison keeps your tone from becoming a *monotone*. They flow subtly but effectively through the best creative articles. They are almost essential to articles of controversy or advice. To achieve them: once again, if appropriate to your subject, acknowledge the opposition.

Then compare and contrast: desirable with undesirable; past with present; people, attitudes, customs, or whatever you are discussing. In short, by putting any two opposites in juxtaposition or by showing variations of the same thing.

People do this all the time (by comparing ourselves with others, for instance). Sometimes comparison makes us miserable, sometimes it spurs us on. Nonetheless, it is inescapable. Articles from the heart are actually a reflection of life; comparison is so natural a method I marvel that so many would-be writers fail to use it.

Watch for it as you read published articles. Slight as it may seem, it is there for a purpose. Comparison and contrast enhance the point and enliven the theme.

As mentioned earlier, it is the lifeblood of the controversial article. You can't be *for* or *against* something without comparing both sides of the issue — and acknowledging the opposition. For examples, see the two I discussed in chapter 7.

The article praising Christmas letters starts off with the merry admission that "Christmas letters have gotten a bad press lately. . . . Well, let the scoffers scoff, the Scrooges sneer—" to us they're great. The article then presents the rewards of writing such letters and keeping them for your family, in contrast to the easier job of just signing and sending cards.

In *A Mother Speaks Up for Censorship*, it's obvious from the first sentence that this will shock some people: "As a writer, I never thought I'd be asking for censorship . . . a word considered worse than murder or mayhem. . . ." Thus the opposition is established—and referred to as the article proceeds with its contrasts: moral and immoral books and movies; public attitudes past and present; liberty gone wild versus responsibility and common sense.

Comparison and contrast are self-evident in writing nostalgia. How things used to be, so different from life today. They can also be very effective in writing about marriage and children, or any of your personal experiences. Differences in personalities, backgrounds, character traits abound. Comparison and contrast weave the various arguments and facets of the piece together. They enable you, the author, to enhance your point and enliven your tone. Watch for them in published articles; mark the places with "CC" or whatever you choose. Then study your own manuscript to see where you can put comparison and contrast to work for you.

Color

Black-and-white television was wonderful when it first came out. But it's hard to imagine being satisfied with even black-and-white snapshots now. The world is all around us in living color, and the eye is equipped to enjoy it. So too is the mental eye. And while countless very fine articles are published in simple black and white, a touch of color adds pleasure to the picture.

Shortly after the death of the famous novelist John P. Marquand, I read a description of him in the *Saturday Review*. It was so vivid and colorful I have used it as a perfect example ever since.

> His were the bluest eyes I have ever seen and they became bluer when he was amused. . . . His eyes seemed the bluer, and his care-

fully combed white hair the whiter and his dark eyebrows the blacker because of the accentuating pinkness of his skin, which in explosive moments could become poppy-red. . . .

It is as if, among all the other beautifully phrased characteristics, we were suddenly seeing the man himself "in living color."

In the personal essay or the nostalgic article (or almost anywhere else) opportunities for color abound. Don't just wrap a blanket around the baby — dye it yellow. When the frost is on the pumpkin, make it an orange pumpkin and the youngster who's carrying it up the hill clad in blue jeans or a red mackinaw. Be careful, of course, not to overdo this; color isn't something to be recklessly splashed around. But if you've written a good piece in black and white and want to brighten it up, go over it with a careful paintbrush. You'll be surprised at how many places there are where a touch of color, like a touch of humor, will make it glow.

Characterization

Articles from the heart depend upon anecdotes, which involve people. You don't have to characterize as you do in writing fiction; there is simply no space to go deeply into motivation or to add much description. But your work has an extra dimension and appeal if you make your people genuine individuals when you can. Just as in fiction, people *do* characterize themselves by what they say, and how they act or look. The trick of the creative writer is to compress this into a few words. For instance, in "Romance vs. The Boss":

> My first boss was a terrifying bully with a heart of ice cream. He looked and sounded like Tarzan to the quaking girl about to test her high school shorthand and typing on his murderously complex dictation. . . . He raged and stormed and scolded, we both suffered. But later, when it was over, he'd mop his scarlet face and grin sheepishly, "Sorry. I think both of us need a milk shake. How about it?" It was the nearest I ever got to the legendary romantic shenanigans at the office.

In a more serious article, "Little One Late":

Dr. James took off his glasses and hesitated before he told me—but I read the news in his sweet gray eyes. He knew I didn't want this baby. "I predict it will be a great blessing to you." He rose, a gentle, snowy-haired giant almost looking like a prophet as he came around the desk to comfort me. "Oh, I bet you tell that to everybody," I wailed. "I sure do." His laugh rang out, even as he patted my shoulder. "And I'm always *right!*"

Opportunities for characterization are plentiful in humorous articles. And the ability to draw vivid characters is important to articles of reminiscence and personal experience. It's less important elsewhere, but since articles from the heart are akin to fiction, you'll find them more fun to write if you characterize briefly where you can. This gives your work that extra quality that lifts it out of the ordinary.

Timeliness

Writers of articles from the heart deal with eternal truths. We do *not* have to keep one step ahead of the news, as journalists do, or deal with current issues and events in the same manner as fact writers. Human emotions (love, hate, fear, anxiety, joy, sorrow) and many human experiences never go out of date. Neither do human problems, even such common ones as worrying (and fighting) about money or just making the best of what you have. But the writer's *approach* to an article from the heart in whatever topic he chooses must be thoroughly modern.

For instance, it would be pretty silly to deal with the perennial question of money in terms of the Great Depression—unless you are carefully comparing experiences from that period to those many people face today: Should a family go bankrupt to put the children through college? How can we manage the staggering cost of a hospital stay? Today's lifestyles—working wives, live-ins, single parents—have brought a whole new *background* to money matters, even though the same old anxieties, hopes and dreams, and misunderstandings about money still exist.

Concerning style and vocabulary, if a word or phrase of current slang will help highlight your point or vitalize your writing, by all means use it. (Even if it too will soon be out of date.) But don't *backdate* your article with Victorian language (" 'twas," "the lad informed me," etc.), or slang already grown quaint with age, or merely sophomoric phrases like "oh, yeah?" or "boy, oh boy!"

An otherwise good article can be ruined by has-been comparisons and illustrations. The article I spoke of, about the wife who fought with waitresses, was dated in this manner: The waitress bellowed "in a voice like Tarzan," and "Joe Louis would have been intimidated." The author mentioned Amy Vanderbilt, Johnny Weismuller, Sonja Henie — names famous in their day, but no longer immediately recognizable. When you're writing for modern readers, you must use names that are making headlines *now* if you want to get attention.

An article should sound timely in all its aspects. Yet for some curious reason many writers, even young ones, reach *back* for their comparisons and examples. This is great if you are writing nostalgia — then your illustrations ought to come straight from grandma's attic. You are intentionally establishing datedness. But in all other instances the writer should sound as modern as possible. Celebrities change, and so do skirt lengths, dances and popular songs. Even computer jargon is not the same as it was a few years ago when computers were new.

A good article can be made better by references to *contemporary* figures, styles, fads, controversies and issues and events on the present scene. They will give readers a start of recognition. They will feel that you are "with it," and so are they, and they enjoy that identification.

Specifics

Articles from the heart are based upon the intangible — ideas. To make those ideas graphic, we pin them down with specifics. We give specific illustrations. We often give the characters in those illustrations specific characteristics and callings. Then, as we attempt to demonstrate the basic premise, we go a step further, adding color and interest through more specifics.

Here is an example, taken from an article in which I challenged the popular notion that you're a bad parent if you don't participate in all your children's activities:

General

I was finally cured of this idea. When people think they can always count on you for all the work, some may be impressed, but mostly you just get blamed.

Specific

The penalties of being little old Mr. or Mrs. Dependable, who can always be counted on to *run the school bazaar, chaperone the dances* and *haul the uniformed troops and tribes* to their supposedly beneficial destinations, can far outweigh the values. . . . The absolute height of some people's reactions is to murmur, "My goodness, I just don't see how she does it," as they *reach for another nibble of salted nuts* and *reflect on their bridge hands.*

Often you are blamed for everything that goes wrong. "See here, my child was *twenty minutes late getting home from Bluebirds* and we always *eat at six.*" Or, "*Jimmy got sick* after the *church picnic.* It does seem to me that those in charge could have *made sure the potato salad was fresh.*"

I have italicized the specifics to make them stand out here. The published version was more effective because it has more feeling and avoided generalizations.

Here are two treatments of my nostalgic article, "Whatever Happened to Run, Sheep, Run?"

General

I often wonder whatever happened to the games we used to play after supper as children. And where are the youngsters who used to enjoy them so much? I suppose they're all grown up now, like me, and their children tease to go out and play, just as we did.

Specific

Whatever happened, I sometimes wonder, to Hide-and-Seek? And Pump, Pump, Pull-Away and Old Gray Wolf? And where are the children who used to trample gardens, clamber over fences, and shatter the quiet darkness with their cries of "Run, Sheep, Run!" They're now suburban housewives, like me, I suppose, or busy, commuting dads. And their offspring are just as eager as we were to play out-of-doors after supper. You can hear them now at their games of kickball in the street. And they're mad about something called Muck-a-Ny. But Hide-and-Seek? Old Gray Wolf? And *what* was Run, Sheep, Run?

Generalized writing may be adequate; and if you are producing essays for profoundly thoughtful literary journals (and your style is otherwise impressive) it may even be preferred. But if you are aiming for popular magazines, be definite. Make choices. Don't simply plant flowers — put them in window pots and decide on geraniums (or petunias); don't have a wife merely cook a husband's favorite dish — decide (even as she must) which dish it shall be. Pot roast? Shrimp Creole or cheese fondue? It doesn't matter; what does matter is that *you* serve the reader a definite image.

It is these details, small but colorful and concrete, that give the article from the heart a plus factor, another extra to help it sell.

Memory Devices

One day my son came home from Coast Guard boot camp full of enthusiasm about a lecturer he had heard. "He was marvelous," he said. "He made us realize so many things I hadn't thought of and that I'll never forget. He put it in terms that hit home with this group of mine stressing what he called 'The Four M's' — Manhood, Money, Matrimony, and wound up with Message: 'Is your life going to be a message or a mess?'"

I was really taken by surprise. Here was a young man who usually pulled down his mental shades at lectures, who didn't even care about books. Yet, he had not only listened, but he was quoting words he felt would influence him all his life. This speaker had recognized how amorphous abstract ideas are, unless they are made vivid through graphic illustrations that etch the ideas into the minds of the audience. He had succeeded with an old but simple memory device: Alliteration and repetition.

I had already read and written hundreds of idea articles, but not until that moment did it dawn on me that this is what good writers and speakers do continually. By accident or deliberate design, we seek to make our thoughts easier to follow and, hopefully, harder to forget. And very often this is accomplished by some small but effective memory device.

Methods

Going through my own published articles, and a great many others, I discovered that memory device methods vary and most of them are not really unique. But the fact that they are used so frequently proves their worth.

Here's what I mean:

1. Enumerating

A list of rules or suggestions numbered 1. 2. 3. This is a good way to organize and write an article; or a good way to summarize. It also qualifies as a memory device.

2. Alphabetizing or alliteration

3. The acrostic (making the first letter of the first word of key paragraphs spell out your point)

I used this device in one of my early published pieces, "Seven Ways to Spell Husband" — Helpfulness, Understanding, etc. Later, I did a parallel piece, "Four Ways to Spell Wife." This was very gimmicky, and I don't recommend it except for beginners who are trying their wings. This device does show, however, how a little trick can help you organize your material and make it clear and concise — and memorable.

4. The symbol

We find symbols used constantly in novels, plays and stories. An object, however insignificant in itself, may *mean* something. A teakettle, a jar of roses, a pair of yellow shoes, may stand for something very important to the character and may illustrate some truth. Since the article from the heart is akin to fiction, how logical then that the symbol is often used. Particularly in the Inspirational Essay, Personal Experience article, or article giving Advice.

I used symbols continually during the years I was writing my column, "Love and Laughter," for the Washington, D.C., *Star*. A daughter's first sheer stockings (first step into maturity, dating, a parent's sense of joy and loss); leading children across a busy street (if only you could lead them as safely through the dangers of life ahead); the real meaning of the doormat on your step saying WELCOME. And I have also used symbols in numerous magazine pieces. "The Family Table" symbolized the unity and solidarity of people drawn together, and since this was an antique table, the lives of families in earlier days.

In these examples, the symbol is more than a memory device; it also sparks and fires the original. Begin to think in terms of symbols, and you will find a rich new source of ideas.

Symbols may crop up almost by accident at the beginning or end of an article. This happened in the personal experience piece about our son's catching and stuffing a huge marlin. The fish became his first major trophy. A trophy is important to a child, but to be significant, a trophy has to be won or earned in some way. The article dealt with the humorous complications of amateurs coping with an eight-foot fish, but the message emerged and was driven home by that symbol of the trophy: "The real trophies aren't the ones you can pay for with money."

5. Dialogue. Questions and answers.

More and more fact writers are using tape recorders for interviews, which they skillfully edit before publication. Such articles may consist of questions and answers, or simply a discussion between two people on an issue of wide interest and appeal.

These interviews are different from the usual columns of advice in newspapers and magazines. Both are excellent sources from which writers may draw ideas. They consist mainly of the answers by established authorities to questions sent in by readers. But the pattern (question and answer) works well for articles from the heart. The difference is that you, the writer, do not assume the role of an expert. Instead, you set up an interview, real or imaginary, in which you propose a question or issue to be discussed. The "answers" derive from the debate and interplay of ideas and clearly establish the points you want to make in your article. This form avoids a lot of straight exposition, and its brisk, natural conversational style makes your article highly readable.

I did this often in my "Love and Laughter" column, calling it "Dialogues With a Daughter," "Dialogues With a Son" — a husband, a dad, a friend, sometimes, "My Favorite Neighbor Says." For instance (condensed):

> *Daughter*: "Wait, Mom, let me look you over."
>
> *Mom*: "I'm okay, I'm just going to the cleaner's and the post office and the grocery store; I'm in a hurry."
>
> "You must be. You look it!"
>
> Startled, you scan the sloppy jeans and tennis shoes, the worn jacket, take a turn before the mirror. "Well, I admit I'm no Miss Universe, but I don't expect to see anybody important."
>
> "Mother, *everybody's* important. I mean really—you just never know. Let me at least do something about your hair." Firmly she sets you down, picks up a brush; meekly you submit to her ministrations—and her lecture. . . . "It's different with kids, it's the style, but with *parents*?"
>
> "You mean I might embarrass you?"
>
> "Well—a little, not too much. You know you'd really save time by changing. I've noticed clerks wait on you quicker, treat you better."
>
> "I suppose that's true, I just never thought of it."
>
> "Honestly, the things mothers have to learn from daughters!" You both laugh. But later, walking to the car, regroomed, how poised and unhurried you feel. Why, you have all the time in the world.

6. A letter, an ad, a TV commercial, or anything else you can conjure up to make your basic idea more tangible.

My article, "What Became of the Girl He Married?", mentioned earlier, (*Better Homes and Gardens, Reader's Digest*) began like this: "Lost: One gay, sweet bride. Girl who thinks I'm wonderful and tells me so. Chief Characteristic: Appreciation! Ample reward offered by one discouraged guy."

It continued: "Countless men could have composed that ad."

Then, after citing the many areas in which women unwittingly fail our husbands and emphasizing how important it is to show our appreciation, I concluded:

The woman who can rediscover those virtues won't have to worry about romance. She'll have her share of it and something even better — a guy who'll be saying in his heart: *"Found: the girl I married."*

Let me add that when I first wrote "What Became of the Man I Married," (which we also discussed earlier), it created such a stir I decided to show the other side of the picture: that men too crave affection and attention, which women aren't always willing or able to give.

A memory device is simply an extra. It is not necessary to the article from the heart. But once you become aware of its possibilities, you will use it more often. It can be very helpful to you as well as the reader. It helps to stitch together the scattered elements of your article and make them cohesive. And sometimes it will provide you with a lively and logical opening, to which you can tie a logical and impressive ending.

You will not find all the extras discussed here present in all the published articles you read. Yet experience has taught me that the articles most intersting to read and easiest to sell are those that have an ingredient of originality and explicitness, an extra shine, a quality of truly caring on the part of the author. The writer who can "bring to it the rainbow," as my mother used to say.

CHAPTER FIFTEEN

Two More: Good Titles and Quotes

*Y*ou have a sympathetic awareness of people. Your ideas are fresh and plentiful. You write well. You know, through instinct, observation or practice, how to put articles together. In other words, you're like a cook who can prepare a balanced and nourishing meal, but you want to make the dishes more attractive, to add a few garnishes and gourmet touches.

Those extras make a good article better and help it sell. Let's take a close look at two of them — title and quotes — and see how they subtly enhance the flavor and liven up the whole article.

Titles

Some writers say not to worry about titles since the editors will probably change them anyway. That's often the case — and the change isn't always for the better. But a catchy title is important. It's the first thing an editor sees. If your title's an attention-getter, the editor will go on reading, but if you use a dull title, you are at a disadvantage from the start.

How do you come up with intriguing titles? Sometimes you have to work hard to find the right title; other times the title seems to come naturally from your unconscious, along with the idea. And the title may even produce the spark for the focus of the article itself. If you are a truly creative writer, you do a lot of thinking; your concepts of life can often be encapsulated into simple but telling phrases. If you are attuned to listening for these phrases, you'll find your title troubles reduced to a minimum, and any problems you have with getting ideas and *focusing on one aspect* to find a strong angle of interpretation will be minimal, too.

When my husband was a graduate student, a group of us used to get together and we had wonderful parties, playing charades or cards and fixing the cheapest possible foods in amusing ways. Since nobody could afford baby-sitters, children were brought along and put to bed. I didn't consciously decide to write an article about being poor but happy, but one day the phrase *"fun without funds"* popped into my head, and off I flew to write a humorous piece by that name about the imaginative things people can do without spending a lot of money. I recalled, in that article, the days when my mother's ingenuity made our simple Christmas celebrations seem abundant, even when my father was out of a job. I concluded with the point that such experiences are enriching.

It's interesting to note how durable that subject is today, when young people often can't afford the price of baby-sitters. We've all seen them — young mothers with babies on their backs, and fathers leading youngsters by the hand, taking off for dinner parties, picnics, or maybe a lecture at college. Where, to nobody's surprise, the mother may nurse her baby. Or they might just stay home, the way we did, invite the neighbors in and provide our own entertainment.

Again, almost without my consciously thinking about it, the words "five ways to finish an affair" flashed through my mind. At that time, being as naïve as Rebecca of Sunnybrook Farm, I didn't even know what an affair really was! Nonetheless, I wrote an earnest but lively article inventing advice for the woman who wants to discourage the attention of a man. I sold it to a large magazine, and to my complete amazement (and the alarm of my husband) I was deluged with letters from women living far more colorful lives than mine.

But not all titles come unsought, of course. Nor does the basic idea always link itself with the perfect title. I often start off with a working title (anything that reasonably resembles what is to be discussed) or no title at all — then find the right title springing from the article as it is written. When this fails, I walk away from the piece and let my unconscious wrestle with it for a while. Or I take another sheet of paper and write as fast as I can, as many titles as I can. By using free association and a lot of alliteration, I find quite often that an excellent title will come.

If none of this works, and I'm still not satisfied, I sift out what seems to be the best choice.

Here are some examples of the various *kinds* of titles you can use. If you will fix them in mind and review them when you are having title trouble, you can't go too far astray. These types can also serve to stimulate your own article ideas.

Alliterative Titles

Alliteration is the repetition of the initial sound in successive words. If not overdone, it makes your title sing: The following are some I've used: "Passport to Popularity," "The Whys of Working Wives," "Don't Hang Onto Heartbreak," "Men, Money, and Marriage," "Hail to the Head of the House." In *MD* magazine, I recently came across "Demons of Disease," and in a popular magazine, "Turn the Tables on Troubles." The possibilities are infinite, if you give your imagination free reign.

How-To Titles

Everybody wants to know how to get more out of life. And those two little words "how to" are the magic key. If you can legitimately tuck them into your title, you're ahead. But don't cheat; never use them unless the article does provide some specific answers, tips or aids.

Here are some more of mine. (And notice the alliteration as well.) "How to Talk to Your Teens," "How to Banish the Blues," "How to Be a Better Friend," "How to Keep Home Life Happy." Such titles are always welcome in a great many magazines.

Controversial Titles

These are generally titles which have shock value, either because they come out swinging against something a lot of people are already getting fed up with, or they take issue with a popular stand: "Don't Give Me Mother's Day," "I'm Sick of All This Sex," "Never Talk Back to Your Husband," "I Want to Stay Home—and Get Paid," "Togetherness Can Destroy a Marriage," "The Little League Breeds Brats."

And you can use a twist on an old saying, like *"Must* I Go Down to the Sea Again?" "Does the End Justify the Jeans?" *"Don't* You Be My Valentine," "If At First You Don't Succeed—Quit! (And Try Something Else)." Here again the article must justify the title, which cannot be used simply to get attention.

Statement or Advice Titles

Closely akin to the controversial is the title that simply states the premise in forthright terms. In these, the words "do," "don't" or "why" frequently come in handy. Samples I've used for my articles are: "Marriage Isn't a Reform School," "Why Women Can't Talk to Their Husbands," "Why Husbands Can't Talk to Their Wives," "Don't Let People Monopolize You."

A quick look through current magazines on the newsstand or the library will give you innumerable examples: "Some of My Best Friends Are Men" (*McCall's*), "Hope Is Healthy," "If You're On a Diet, Shut Up!" (*Redbook*), "Making Worry Work for You" (*Woman's World*), "Raising Difficult Kids — Rx for Success" (*Woman's Day*), "Fill Your Senses, Light Up Your Life (*Sports Afield*). These "statement titles" often begin with or include a number: "10 Steps . . . ," "Nine Ways to Keep Thin . . . ," "25 Slim-Fast Fashion Tips. . . ." These number titles are found in all kinds of pieces, from advice on how to do almost anything from cooking to building a doghouse or cleaning a rug (a new way, of course!).

Question Titles

You can turn almost every mundane, pedestrian title into a captivating one by putting it into question form: "Can *Anyone* Learn to Swim?" (or ski, cook, hang glide); "Can You and Your Lover Be Friends?" "Should You Always Keep Your Temper?" "What If Your Son Doesn't Like Baseball (and His Father Is an Addict)?"

By using a question title, you also have an excellent cohesive device for the article itself. Put your opening statement in the form of this same question and deal with that question throughout the body of the article. You can then close the article by repeating the question and letting it summarize and clinch your conclusion. For instance: "How important is church? It helped us through the most critical time our family ever faced. It may well be the most important single force for hope and help for you too."

A Catchy Phrase or Sentence

A catchy phrase may make a lively title. It could be a bit of dialogue taken directly from the article or a single sentence. These phrases are especially effective in nostalgia pieces or in the personal essay: "All Doors Led to the Kitchen," "Do You Love Me in the Supermarket?", "Goodbye, Family, Hello, World!" (about the older woman going back to work).

First-Person Titles

If you're writing a personal experience article, your title should be no problem: "I Don't Remember Mama," "We Filmed Our Baby's Birth," "I Know in My Heart My Mother Loved Me," "I Put My Wife on a Diet," "My Husband Feels Like a Failure," "I Grew Up Without Religion." Such titles provide instant impact. They ring true.

Whether the experience is as unique as crossing the Ganges on a crocodile, or as common as trying to get used to a word processor, such titles are attention-getting in their implied, "This happened to me, and here's how I reacted. You'll find it significant, too."

As in all other aspects of the article from the heart, title categories overlap. You'll find that the best ones contain several of the elements cited. Remember that good titles are lively, they have rhythm, and very often contain a vivid noun, adjective or action verb. Bad titles, on the other hand, are those which are vague, downbeat, innocuous, obtuse or just plain dull: "Dread Is Inevitable," "The Rest of the Time," "I Shall Never Forget the Day," "Methods With Children That Are Ineffective." Or those dry pedagogical titles that sound as if they had strayed from somebody's graduate thesis: "Marital Crises vs. Sibling Rivalry." They create the impression that here is a piece that is inept, tired, not quite with it. The writing which follows must be awfully good to overcome the handicap of a poorly chosen title.

Think of your title as a banner — bright, new, snapping in the breeze — instead of an old faded one that wilts and sags and captures nobody's eye.

Quotes

Quotes can be an important extra for many articles of the heart. Not all types, I hasten to add. Humor, nostalgia and sketches usually do nicely without them. But when it comes to articles of advice or controversy, any serious discussions, it helps to have the opinions of recognized authorities. They validate your arguments. They add both charm and substance. Mainly, they keep the whole piece from sounding too "top of the head," and make it authentic.

As a creative writer, you must constantly fight your ego. You may be so fired with your own ideas that you find it hard to make room for anybody else. I used to draw all of my anecdotes from my own experiences or from those of people I knew, or I made them up. I wrote and sold dozens of lively or impassioned articles without consulting references of any sort.

Better Homes and Gardens had published a whole series of my articles on marriage and child care, when the editors discovered I wasn't quoting anybody but myself. They suggested that thereafter I should consult and work in some authoritative quotes.

My first reaction was indignation. "Why should people want a re-hash of what other people think? They want to know what the author thinks!" It was with extreme annoyance and contrary to my better judgment that I trudged to the library to check out all the books I could find on marriage. At first it was pretty dreary going, but I was soon repaid by all the new article ideas that these experts sparked.

Also, it was heartening to discover that many of my pet theories were validated by doctors, psychologists, psychiatrists, social workers and marriage counselors. It was also startling—and valuable—to discover that there was a considerable body of opinion that disagreed with my views. (Here was a good argument for "anticipating the opposition," so important to any article of advice or controversy.) My reading and research made me think my ideas through more deeply.

I don't honestly believe the articles I wrote after this period of research were that much better than the ones I had written previously. But they did fit the growing demand for articles that were "authenticated and based on a firm ground of research and fact." I made the transition to this new approach by first blocking out what I wanted to say, then hunting until I found a suitable passage in a book or professional report that validated my views. If I found none, I moved to a different focus and shifted direction.

Newspapers

I then discovered another excellent source of quotes: newspaper interviews. A celebrity comes to town, and his ideas on life, love and his own success are often quoted. Generally this person will relate anecdotes to illustrate how he got his start, or little incidents that influenced his philosophy. So here you have two possibilities: The quote that will simply flavor and underscore your point: "As Bette Davis once said, 'There's only one thing to do with life when it starts closing in on you—cope with it, dammit.' " Or the appropriate anecdote: "When Bette Davis was six years old her mother sent her to the neighborhood grocery for a pound of butter. It was a hot night, the butter melted, and by the time she got home she was smeared, and the neighborhood kids laughed—."

Daily and Sunday newspapers are filled with such material, especially in the Sunday supplements or the Living and Home departments. And if you read publications like the *Star*, the *Globe*, or the *National Enquirer*, you'll find more than you can use. Some of them have whole columns of "quotable quotes," as *Reader's Digest* calls them in its one-page feature. And don't overlook the obituaries. When a prominent person dies, his biography (which has often been prepared for some time so it will be ready to use on his or her death) is updated as necessary and published in major newspapers. This often includes characteristic quips, statements about important events, anecdotes, and genuinely good quotes. Here, for instance, is part of a yellowed clipping from an AP dispatch on the death of Oscar Hammerstein:

> Mr. Hammerstein was an unabashed sentimentalist and made no bones about it. "I know the world is filled with trouble and many injustices," he once said. "But reality is as beautiful as it is ugly. I think it is just as important to sing about beautiful mornings as it is to talk about slums. I just couldn't write anything without hope in it."

Then followed an anecdote about the time Mae West advised him, "Kid, get out of the theater and be a lawyer. The theater isn't for you. You've got too much class." Watch for such material and when it strikes you, cut it out. File it with your folders of article ideas, or keep a celebrity file. Then when you need a quote or illustration for a special theme, you will have one.

Be a Name-Dropper

Name-dropping may not be good manners in conversation; in articles it's desirable. All the names need not be world-famous, however. (In fact, it's refreshing if they're not — you thereby avoid the overworked episodes, and statements so familiar they've become almost clichés.) They simply must be people who have achieved some distinction, whose opinion can be useful in confirming what you say. Never mind that readers may or may not recognize them; even editors don't know every important person in the world. Just be sure your authorities have the credentials you give them. Careful editors sometimes check.

I once quoted a good friend of mine, Dr. Jonathon Williams, an internationally known neurosurgeon. To the surprise of both of us, he had a call from the editor of *Reader's Digest*, who was considering my piece, to make sure the doctor was who I said he was, and had been quoted accurately. (A few magazines even employ research assistants to check *all* your references. Another time I was asked to verify a little ditty I'd heard in Scotland!) This doesn't happen often, particularly when you've established your own reputation for veracity as a writer, but it's best to be sure. You *can* make up characters to use in your anecdotes; but anyone you quote as an authority must be genuine.

Almost any writer, especially if he lives in or near a city, may know or make contact with some distinguished people. A university president, for instance, a marriage counselor or psychologist, TV personalities, other writers, singers, dancers, artists, athletes, politicians past or present. The list is endless, especially since the names needn't always be that famous. If you happen to know such people personally, it's perfectly legitimate to ask them, "I'm doing an article about solitude," for instance, "getting away from it all — what do you think, and may I quote you?" Or write a letter (always enclosing a stamped, self-addressed envelope), giving a portion of your text, and asking an opinion. Successful people are usually very nice, they like to accommodate if they can; often they're flattered.

Never persist, however, if you don't get a reply. They're probably just too busy—and writers should be too busy to care.

Abundant source material may also be found in classical references. Every writer should have handy on his bookshelf, along with his typewriter, the complete works of Shakespeare, the Bible and as many books of quotations as he can find. Bartlett's *Familiar Quotations* is the best known, but there are many others that are well organized, have contemporary authorities and quotations arranged by subject; they can be very useful to bolster what you are trying to convey in your article. You can often find some little-known but useful volumes of this kind in secondhand bookstores, and in paperback editions that are much less expensive than the original hardbound volumes.

It is often surprising how many seemingly modern quotes you can find in the works of writers of the last century or earlier: Emerson, Lord Chesterfield or other favorites of yours.

They are used in this way: "As Victor Hugo said, 'To reform a man, you must begin with his grandmother.' And true, you can't hope to change basic traits. Nature has fixed those so firmly you must accept any individual pretty much as-is—" ("Marriage Isn't a Reform School"). . . . Or, "Tolstoy declared, 'The woman who marries me must know my most secret thoughts,' and handed his bride his diary. A man as smart as Tolstoy should have known better." ("Do You Dare to Be Honest in Marriage?")

Getting Permission

Now let's summarize the business of permissions:

Books

If you quote from a book, write the publisher and/or author for permission. Short prose quotations used for illustration constitute "fair use," and permission need not be asked. But I think it is both wise and courteous to give the title, author and publisher's name in the text or in a footnote. Of course, books in "public domain" (not still protected by copyright) can be quoted without permission, but again the title, author and publisher should be mentioned. Usually, I don't write for permission where necessary until the article has been accepted. (This saves embarrassment if the article does not make the grade.) What if permission is refused? This is not likely to happen, since publishers want as much mention of the books they publish as they can get. But if permission to quote is denied or the fee requested by them is too high, you may not use the quote in question in any form.

Poems and Songs

It is essential always to ask permission to quote from a song or poem, even a few words, since that would constitute a large proportion of the total work. Music publishers are especially insistent on this point, considering the fact that a single line is often repeated throughout, and represents what could be construed as unfair use of the lyrics, which are, of course, copyrighted. The publisher's name is usually on the sheet music or record. If neither is available, you can find out who owns the copyright through ASCAP or BMI, performing rights organizations. For the address to write, call your music store. Or better yet, pay them a visit. I've only done this a couple of times but found them very helpful, glad to give me the information.

Newspapers and Magazines

Articles in magazines or feature stories in newspapers are also in copyright, and you must write to the paper if more than a few lines are used, and that use must be for the purpose of illustration only.

News stories or published interviews may usually be quoted from without permission, if the quote is short and its purpose is to point up what you are saying in your article. This is also true for published interviews for which you may not in fact be able to track down the reporter or his subject. (Sometimes these interviews do not carry a byline.) If a celebrity is quoted as saying, "Life's tough, but you have to take it," these words are in public domain and you may quote them without permission. If, on the other hand, you want to quote an anecdote that was included in a reporter's hard-to-come-by story, you should ask permission by writing to the paper and give credit to the reporter and the newspaper.

Or write directly to the interviewer (if you know who it is) and say, "That was a great interview. Do you mind if I work it into my article, giving you credit, of course?" If the author (or newspaper) objects, you might try writing to the subject of the interview to ask a question or two that will give you approximately the same response that was quoted in the interview.

Reporters get justifiably upset at having their material used by other writers whose pieces are sometimes only clip-and-paste jobs. *Never* use another writer's words in retelling an anecdote.

If you want to quote from a published speech, write to the person who gave it, rather than to the newspaper or the reporter who covered it. By doing so, you will probably get a complete copy of the text and other data as well.

Friends and Acquaintances

You don't have to get permission from anyone, unless you use his name. But it's very important to do so if you're quoting a doctor.

I know all this sounds complicated and a lot of trouble. It really isn't. Articles from the heart, by their very nature, don't require much validation from important people. But when an appropriate quote will enhance your message, use it. It will be a bonus. Most of the time quotes almost drop into your lap, you don't have to track them down. And if you keep them short (no more than fifty words) you don't have to ask for permission.

CHAPTER SIXTEEN

Twelve Secrets of Style

Style is that elusive element in writing that some people say cannot be taught. Fundamentally, I agree. Like rhythm or good taste or passion, if you have to explain to somebody what it *is*, then don't bother; he probably doesn't have it.

Yet the truly creative writer (and the only one who should try articles from the heart), *can* be shown definite ways to improve his own style.

Just what *is* style? Whether or not you need the following definition, I want to share my concept of it. This is my definition of style:

> The art of clear, effective and readable writing. The rhythm that makes a sentence sound right to the mental ear. The ruthless cutting out of phrases that only clutter and impede this special music. And always, always, the patient, painstaking search for the perfect combination of words and phrases that will create this mental music and express what is to be said in the most moving and effective way.

Style is important. Of style, Aristotle said, "It is not enough to know what to say; we must also say it in the right way." The first impression an editor gets from any piece of writing is the author's style. The subject may be a good one, the words sufficient — like clothes, they may *cover* it; but if they are sloppy, prosaic or dull, or merely inappropriate, the editor has to drive himself to get through the manuscript.

How to Develop Style

Any definition of style leaves room for infinite variations. Style is a matter of taste, hence there is no absolute. No one is qualified to say that this, and only this, is the proper way to express anything. The style of some writers is blunt, terse, staccato. The style of others may be brisk, blithe, full of caprice. The style of still others may flow. Sometimes a writer uses one effect so consistently it is possible to identify his work without a byline.

Most writers vary their style, using some or all of the foregoing effects to suit their material, although generally one style — cadences, individualities of expression — will predominate.

In short, your style is *your* way of writing. Usually it forms slowly over the years, colored by your own maturing and by the unconscious absorbing of words, phrases, meters, expressions, both oral and written. Particularly by the conscious or unconscious imitation of the rhythms and techniques of the material you most often read.

Now maturing means not simply growing older, but growing in awareness, in depth, and in our critical faculties. Very often the books which enthralled us in our youth strike us in our middle years as unbelievably bad. Our own early writing efforts now sometimes turn our stomachs. How *could* I have been so inept, so pompous or so wordy? (For this very reason I advise saving everything you write; it will show you how much you have improved.) Again, the truly creative writer often finds some of his earlier work astonishingly good. This, too, is excellent for the ego; it confirms the fact that the talent was always there, and worthy of your continuing labor, determination and sacrifice.

Frequently, a writer's later works don't equal his or her early successes. This is especially true of novelists, even very famous ones of the recent past and also writers whose books are classics. But the writer of short forms, such as articles from the heart, need not worry about going into a style decline. It's like playing the piano — the more you practice, the more effortless and polished your performance will become.

This, then, is a cardinal rule. *You must write!* Not just occasionally, but regularly, if you are to develop style.

Style is also developed through *awareness of the style of others.*

It is no accident that most writers are avid readers. If you are truly creative, reading stirs the spirit of your own creativity. Ideas begin to beat their wings, phrases to sing; you often must stop reading and fly to the typewriter to write. (For this reason, paradoxically, the most prolific writers are not as widely read as many nonwriters who aren't inhibited by these interruptions.) When this happens you are generally moved to write in the mood or style of the work that has excited you.

In fact, you can develop certain aspects of your style more quickly and effectively if you will intentionally expose yourself to the kind of things you want to write. If you're going to write humor, steep yourself in humor. Read it particularly just before you sit down to write. The same goes for more thoughtful pieces. Put the unconscious to work, as I suggested earlier; let it absorb the mood, the pace, the tone. Then when you get to the typewriter, you are warmed up and ready to go. You'll get off to a faster start and write more fluently, and better.

Now this is far different from a conscious imitation of anyone else's style. Read widely in the field of your favorites, instead of reading any single writer too much. Otherwise your work will be full of echoes. Imitative writers only sound like poor carbon copies of the writers they try to emulate. Truly creative writers should work to develop a style that is uniquely their own, even though every writer who is honest, no matter how distinguished, will acknowledge that his style has been influenced by writers before him. And generally it is an amalgam; into the deep well of his unconscious have poured the word patterns of many authors he has admired — no two of them really alike, but all of this fused and forged by the flame of his own genius, to emerge as the style that most suitably expresses the things that his spirit demands.

In developing style, however, one should *consciously take note* of how other good writers achieve their effects. Train yourself to be aware. Mark passages that please you and reread them, searching out why. Underscore colorful figures of speech, taste their particular flavor, pay special attention to rhythms.

For years I trained myself to read with a deliberate consciousness of rhythms. When I found an author whose work I admired, I would read his or her work, feeling consciously, unconsciously and emotionally the sure and delicate balance of the phrasing. I could in some cases almost have measured them with a metronome. "Rhythm! Notice the rhythm," I would write in the margin of each page where I was particularly struck by it. This is the way a writer who really cares about style develops. He always listens and is aware of it in the writing of others. Consciously and unconsciously, he tries to learn and improve from the *best* that he can find.

Writers of the best creative articles very often have a talent for fiction, too. But whether you want to write fiction or nonfiction, the best way to improve your style is to read the great novelists — Willa Cather, Thomas Wolfe, Dickens — whoever appeals to you, from whatever period. Read your favorites over and over, mark the passages that stir you, study their style.

This approach, along with writing practice, is the surest way to develop your style.

Secrets of Style

Let's look now at some specific suggestions for improving style.

1. Be simple. Write so that "all who run may read."

Somerset Maugham said the important elements in writing are "clarity, simplicity, euphony and liveliness." Clarity and simplicity, notice. For writing is communication. And certainly in the article from the heart we must say what we mean in the most direct and simple, if (we hope) engaging way. But this admonition applies to any form of writing.

I do not consider obscurity the mark of profundity. A good mind with a good idea should strive to make that idea understood. When the author chooses instead to bury it in verbiage, convoluted sentences, and references of such erudition that even the erudite get lost, he is not communicating; he is showing off. Or he is camouflaging an idea that wasn't worth all the mental acrobatics.

Rudolf Flesch has a fine time with this sort of thing in his delightful book *The ABC of Style — A Guide to Plain English*, which he also subtitles, "A word diet for the verbally overweight." This book, published some years ago, is still in demand by people who want to improve their writing and speaking style. It is recommended reading, especially for those who have fallen in love with their own professional jargon. Jargon has no place in the article from the heart. Yet when clergymen, educators, government workers, psychologists, etc., attempt articles for mass circulation they often find themselves unwilling or unable to speak the language of laymen. Here, for example, are some excerpts from a would-be article for parents by a woman who teaches child psychology at a large university:

> The adolescent is very anxious to conform to the peer group. When the peer group proposes behavior that may be alien to behavior patterns considered acceptable at home, the adolescent undergoes severe emotional strain. This may be unapparent to parents whose primary objectives are to meet the child's physical and material needs as dictated by their own peer groups, yet who fail to comprehend the child's resultant motivational conflicts as reflected in standards evolving within the framework. . . .

Such pedantry is not only straight from Dullsville, it isn't even clear.

To improve your style, let your work cool off a few days after you have it down on paper. Then reread, searching out every sentence that may be fusty, pompous, turgid or too complex — that does not say exactly what you mean. This does not mean that you cannot be subtle, or artful, or that you must be blunt or "write down." Only that you must be clear. And the more simple and clear you are, the lovelier your writing style will become.

2. Avoid trite phrases and clichés.

Trite phrases or figures of speech are the kiss of death to any manuscript. And that "kiss of death" is exactly what is meant by a cliché: Any group of words that has become hackneyed and stale from overuse.

In the article from the heart, as in any piece of writing, the style must, of course, sound natural. We use the vernacular, we toss in commonplace phrases, an occasional slang expression, to achieve that quality of "liveliness" Maugham mentioned (as opposed to the textbookish horror cited). But the writer who does this knows what he's doing; he is not leaning on a creaky old cane of clichés because he is mentally too lazy or enfeebled to think of anything better.

A pleasing style is a matter of continuing originality — not freakish, not way out, but a constant inventiveness on the part of the author, who seeks always to present his thoughts in combinations that are fresh, arresting, filled with little surprises. The reader may not be aware of this at all; he may not have the slightest idea why one writer charms him, another does not. It is just one of those subtle secrets of style that the accomplished writer masters through practice and observation (along with his own talent) and then forgets he's using.

The very first step in achieving this inventiveness is to go through every manuscript, ruthlessly cutting every obvious cliché.

Figures of speech such as: "a carpet of grass," "cool as a cucumber," "rich as Croesus," "light as a feather, soft as butter, hard as nails." The time-weary adage, epigram, phrase or quotation: "Ours not to reason why, ours but to do or die." "Man cannot live by bread alone." "While there's life there's hope." "Man brings home the bacon." Any combinations of words that are trite: "The day of reckoning," "staunch friend," "careworn hands," "face facts," "call a spade a spade," "cry from the rooftops."

An *occasional* use of common figures and phrases may lend just the homey, forthright touch you need, and it's impossible to avoid them altogether; but generally speaking they should be avoided.

A sure cure for clichés is to put them to work for you. Twist them around, change even *one word*, and the phrase will have the ring of familiarity while producing surprise.

Here's how it works with similes and metaphors. If "dry as a rope" turns up in an article, we snap to attention. A rope *is* dry and far livelier an image than the dreary old "bone" a lazier writer would have settled for. "Cool as a Popsicle" is more colorful than "cool as a cucumber." And instead of "a carpet of grass," make it "a wall-to-wall carpet of grass — the neighbor's wall and ours."

Or change one word in any familiar saying: "Man cannot live by martinis alone." "You can lead a kid to water, but you can't make him think." "You need that advice like you need a hole in your typewriter." "If at first you don't succeed, quit!"

Or twist the tail of your cliché for a double effect: "Man may bring home the bacon, but his wife still has to cook it." In a light article I did about women's spending habits: "Ours not to reason why, ours but to buy and buy."

The unwitting use of clichés is the mark of the amateur; the professional writer uses them only deliberately.

3. Make your figures of speech appropriate.

Figures of speech, like anecdotes, are a natural, almost inescapable form of human discourse. Listen to any speaker, in public or private, and the comparisons pop out: "She's a big cow of a woman." "Marriage is like a superhighway: once you get on it's sometimes impossible to get off." "Now take this clock; if I were to break it and try to put it back together, I'd have the same kind of mess we're facing now—" "The cartilage between these vertebrae is tough but soft—like a sausage, or a cushion." People talk this way all the time, even prosaic people; it's one way to make ourselves understood. And the more colorful the person, the more colorful and apt his comparisons usually are.

When it comes to writing, there are authors who develop an excellent style without ever using figures of speech. But for most creative writers, imagery—new similes and metaphors—is a source of pleasure and will add not only color to the script, but also clarity. And when such figures of speech are appropriate to the background material, they intensify that material, tie the whole piece neatly together, and add cohesiveness.

To illustrate this from some of my own articles and stories: An architect sees the sky as a vast blueprint, the trees as the strong timbers of a building. To an interior decorator hills are "upholstered in the gaudy colors of autumn." To a seamstress the spring earth is "needlepointed in fine little stitches of green." Rain does not dance on a roof for a stenographer, to her it is typing; it would be tap-dancing if the character or background were in a dancing studio. In an article about garden clubs I referred to "a bouncing bouquet of women whose own petals might be fading, but whose stems were still sturdy and whose roots were green." I used verbs like "pluck, cut, dig, gather achievements in a basket." "Enthusiasm runs dry and has to be watered."

By using a little free association, you will find some delightful figures will present themselves to you. And when figures of speech are drawn directly from the background material, they accomplish three things: give unity to the article, emphasize your point, add sparkle to your style.

4. Don't mix figures of speech.

Better no images at all than mixed ones. This does not mean that you must use only one figure of speech, even in variation, throughout the article or story. That would be monotonous. What I mean is that they should be in reasonable harmony with the subject, the background, and each other, and that two or more cannot be allowed to fight it out in the same sentence or paragraph.

Here is a grim example: "These rules and regulations, which seemed at first to be an open gate to freedom, would soon boomerang into a leering monster." In the first place, rules by their very nature are restricting; the *last* thing they normally would suggest is an open gate. But even if they did somehow represent a gate, that gate could not boomerang, and that boomerang could not become a monster. Here we have three totally divergent images, as unalike as possible, and the result is not only bad writing, it is nonsense. It confuses instead of clarifies.

5. Avoid rare, difficult words (but don't throw your thesaurus away).

Obscurity is not, I repeat, a sign of erudition. And the deliberate use of long mouthfilling words calculated to impress the reader is more likely to irritate him. When I wrote my first novel I was very eager to sound erudite. Accordingly, I cluttered it up with remote classical references and never used a simple word where a blockbuster would do. Good editing eliminated most of this, but a few remained, and I remember being actually flattered when one of the most learned women in Pittsburgh called me to say she had consulted all her dictionaries and still couldn't find a certain word. I should have been ashamed.

On the other hand, there is simply no excuse for being word poor. Your dictionary and your thesaurus offer a dazzling banquet of words, all free, all yours. And the truly creative writer is or should be a word hound, hungry for more. "That's a good word," you'll hear him exclaim in conversation, "why don't I use that more often?" Not a rare or unusual word necessarily, but merely a *good* word that has somehow failed to make itself at home in his general vocabulary.

6. Seek always for the right, the perfect word.

The truly creative writer cares deeply about words — enough to take infinite pains to make his writing style as nearly perfect as possible. This means a constant quest to find the one word that most precisely expresses his thought. Here his thesaurus is invaluable. He knows that somewhere in it lurks that word. Occasionally he is baffled, he fails to find it. To proceed he may have to substitute; even so, consciously and unconsciously his mind continues its quest until suddenly, in the middle of the night perhaps, the right word soars to the surface. Good writing can come only from this quality of deep caring, and this willingness to work toward perfection. Bad writing comes sometimes less from lack of talent than from sheer carelessness. You have to know what a word really *means* before you can use it properly. Yet many would-be writers snatch at a word that reasonably resembles the one they think they want. The result is like the singer who doesn't quite hit the note. So suddenly and unexpectedly sour, it can be hilarious. Or it's like the person whose dialogue is entertaining because of its comical near-misses. We once had a laundry man whose weekly appearance I eagerly anticipated because of remarks like this: "The house was absolutely *infatuated* with bedbugs!" "We always wanted children but my wife had a misconception."

7. Don't repeat key words (unless for emphasis or effect). Two glaring signs of the amateur are the prevalence of clichés and word repetitions. The first thing I do is to delete them from the manuscript. Any good editor preparing a work for publication will do the same — unless, of course, the repetitions are deliberate, to achieve a desired effect, to build momentum, as in the case of what is called "incremental repetition," where the force of what is being said grows with each repeated use (usually not more than three).

I once heard a well-known children's editor pooh-pooh this by showing how Lincoln used repetition in his Gettysburg Address. "Suppose he had said —

> But in a larger sense we cannot dedicate, we must not consecrate, we are unable to hallow this ground. The brave men, living and deceased who passed away here, have immortalized it far above our poor powers —

Doesn't that sound ridiculous?" she asked.

Of course, because the analogy was off base. Lincoln, that master stylist, knew exactly what he was up to. He was *intentionally* using repetition for cadence and emphasis. This is very different from using the same word over and over because the author is so mentally impoverished or so lazy that he can't produce a synonym.

Some writers who are making progress still seem absolutely blind to their constant repetitions. I once rewrote a book for a talented woman with a great life story to tell. But that story had been hopelessly bogged down with verbiage—some of it very nice indeed, but most of it cliché-ridden and swamp-deep in repetition.

For instance, she would use a certain word, like *wall*, incessantly. There were walls between people, stone walls of resistance, walls to build, walls to be chipped away. *World* was another overused word: the world of the mentally ill, private worlds, worlds to learn, worlds to conquer. Week after week I would tear down those "walls" and try to find substitutes for those "worlds" and urge, "Don't repeat!" And when the next chapter came back it too would be heavy with walls, worlds, and other key words which kept bumping into each other, often in the same sentences. Either such people have an idea that individual style is something you're stuck with and can't or shouldn't be improved, or they are quite literally incapable of seeing—or hearing—their faults.

All of us have blind spots when it comes to repetitions. I always let my work cool off, then go over it carefully to find them. But they are like printer's errors: no matter how diligently you read a proof, to your dismay they still pop up. One *Reader's Digest* editor has said that this comes about because the mind, having just presented you with a satisfactory word, feeds it right back to you again, and you snatch it and race on unaware of it. If you are pleased with the total effect, your mind may not register the repeated word even on rereading.

But the conscientious writer *cares* about his style sufficiently to stop the offender if he can. I remember once waking in the middle of the night to realize that I had used "shelter" on two successive pages. The next day I called the editor, had her get out the script and change the second to "protection," which was equally descriptive.

If the repetition is used *intentionally* to achieve emphasis or cadence, it is legitimate. Lincoln knew this. It is the careless, unnecessary repetitions that clutter your style and that editors deplore.

8. Watch out for redundancy.

Here is another big offender. A redundancy in basic argument is simply belaboring the obvious, repeating the point needlessly. A redundancy in style uses two words or statements of the same meaning together in sentences or paragraphs:

"The children could cross the street safely and not get hurt."

"Evidently the ostensible purpose was —"

"He was a short fat man, quite heavy and overweight."

9. Discover alliteration.

Alliteration adds flow and loveliness to style. It makes your writing sparkle, it smooths the rough edges, it causes a page to perk up, a sentence to sing. Alliteration comes naturally to some writers, others seem totally unaware of it. Yet it is so simple a device for achieving harmony and grace in writing that I marvel more people don't use it.

Like anything else, alliteration must be applied with a deft and careful hand. Overdo it and you're dead: "The light leaped nimbly over the limpid lake." "They jumped to the conclusion that just to join would be to get justice." Alliteration does not mean tongue-twisters or fancy frills. Nor is it merely the dumb thump of words that contain the same syllables: "It will be apparent to the parents." "The man was confounded when he found the wallet." "I don't understand how he stands it."

Rather, alliteration is a combination of words that may or may not begin with the same letter, but whose sounds echo each other, sometimes in the body of the word. And to be truly pleasing, good alliteration joins hands with rhythm. Let's see which is more effective in the following example, "Take Time for Christmas Memories," an article I wrote for *Better Homes and Gardens*, which also appears in the book *At Christmas the Heart Goes Home*, a Doubleday Treasury of my Christmas writings.

It is the day before Christmas. The cookies are crisp in the kitchen and the last late cards have been mailed. The sleigh bells on the door make clamorous music each time the children dash in and out. Then suddenly they are gone, the lot of them, husband and all, on those mysterious, last-minute errands they always remember in the late afternoon. Except for a radio carol and the contented crackling of the fire before which our big dog dreams, I am alone in a house gone still.

As you see, there are three T sounds in the title: Take, Time, Christmas; and four M's: Time, Christmas, Memories. . . . In the second sentence, four C sounds: cookies, crisp, kitchen, cards. And the first three L's: last, late, mailed. The L's continue to flow throughout the paragraph, and the C's and M's chime in: sleigh bells, clamorous music, children, last minute, late, crackling . . . "alone in a house gone still." Plus little grace notes of B's and D's: "before which our big dog dreams."

If we take out the alliteration we also remove most of the melody: "I'd baked the cookies, and mailed all our cards out. There were sleigh bells on the door. They were noisy as the children ran in and out. Their dad showed up and took everybody away on errands. The fire was burning, the dog was asleep. The radio was playing, but the house seemed quiet by myself."

The article was written so long ago I have no idea how my original, rough draft version read. But I'll bet I rewrote that passage several times, plucking and replucking the strings of alliteration until it brought the most pleasure to my own musical ear. Not until your writing pleases *you* should you ever send it out in the hope of pleasing somebody else.

Let alliteration go to work for you. It will help to resolve your title problems. It will smooth out those balky sentences and add a few feathers to your writing wings.

10. Keep sentences as short as possible.

Some sentences demand more length than others. But long sentences tend to become involved, convoluted, complex. Study all your sentences carefully to make sure they cannot be improved through shortening. Delete unnecessary phrases. Or break the sentence up. Remember that readability depends a lot upon simplicity. And style, particularly in the creative article, must above all be readable.

11. Develop you inner ear for rhythm.

Read both with your eye and your inner ear. The writer who is conscious of style does this continually, mentally measuring the cadences of other writers, registering the variations they have used.

Here are some article openings that I have saved for years because of the sheer rhythmic charm of their style:

"Youth, they say, lives for the future, old age in the past. And the middle years? I do myself doubt whether youth takes more account for the future than can be colored by the mood of a day" ("Mental Annuity," an essay by Elizabeth Bowen). Or Constance Foster's "If I Had a Daughter, I'd Tell Her This" (*Ladies' Home Journal*): "They told me, the old ones did when I was young, that childbearing was a sorrow and a pain."

Because of my own aesthetic makeup, sentences like that touch me emotionally and send me into a kind of spiritual waltz. I like their *beat*. You may enjoy cadences of a totally different kind. Very well, note them, mark them, clip them, read them aloud. In so doing you will be making a small but deep impression upon your writing style.

12. Don't be afraid to be original. Give your writing wings!

The truly creative writer of articles from the heart or anything else, cannot bear to be just like anybody else. Like Daedalus, he has a positive compulsion to fashion wings of his own and fly. And it is this quality of originality that sends him soaring above the ordinary. In several senses of the word, he gives not only himself but his editor and reader a lift.

This does not mean that you should strain and struggle to be cute or shocking or freakish. Only that you will not settle for the hackneyed, the mundane. Scan every page of every manuscript asking: How can I say this in a better way? Where can I add a bit of stardust, make it sparkle, make it shine? Sometimes you can't, the material itself has so much to do with style. But no matter how serious your message, you do *not* need to sound dull, sluggish, thick-tongued, tired. If you do, you are simply in the wrong business. Certainly you should not try the article from the heart.

How to achieve this originality? Like style itself, originality is a matter of talent and instinct; unless you have a dash of it within you it cannot really be taught. But there are ways whereby your native gifts can be enhanced and your attitudes improved. As I've already suggested, turn your clichés around (you can do this even in serious articles sometimes). You can do more with alliteration. You can create fresh figures of speech. You can even invent new words.

The more you write, the more ways you will discover to put the touch of individuality upon your writing, to give it wings.

Style, your style, *can* be improved. And once you reach the point of caring very much indeed about your style, you will enjoy the act of writing. You will feel the almost sensual pleasure that comes from creating effects with words.

CHAPTER SEVENTEEN

Methods and Markets

*I*n this book we have talked a lot about readers. And how to write the warm, human, articles from the heart that so many people need and want. But almost nothing about the only way to *reach* those readers, which is actually getting published. Because what earthly good is an article on *any* subject, no matter how skillfully written, if its fate is only to lie in a desk drawer, unread? To me that's not only foolish and fruitless, but selfish. Remember the inspiring words of that teacher I spoke of in the beginning: "You must write beautiful things for people who crave beautiful things."

For people, note. Not for yourself alone. If you are learning to write better, you should also learn the sheer mechanics of producing a manuscript and finding a publisher for it, so your work can be read.

In this chapter I'm going to explain some of my own methods of writing and selling these articles. Also, to answer a lot of questions that are often hurled at me during teaching sessions. The answers may or may not match those that another writer might give. But this is how writing and selling articles from the heart works for me.

The Actual Writing

1. Do you outline?

Only in the sense of putting on paper every idea pertinent to the subject that occurs to me. This may include whole passages or paragraphs that may be used, or merely fragments, phrases, suggested thoughts or approaches. This outline, if you can call it that, goes into a Manila folder, where supplementary material can be tossed.

The folder, labeled with a tentative title, is filed, alphabetically, where I can find it easily.

I have learned to use good strong paper for this outline (or for anything used in notebook or journal) rather than cheap yellow second sheets which wear out easily (your notes may age a long time before you need them); also to write on only one side of the paper. If you try to put down on the back ideas for other articles, you can't file properly, and even ideas pertinent to this particular article may be forgotten or lost.

2. When is the best time to write the article?

When you're excited about it. Thus the rough outline you start may grow into the completed manuscript before the day is over. Or it may have to wait until a new and urgent style or approach occurs to you.

I think it is a good idea to write as much of the actual article as you can at the first sitting, but never in the sense of, "I am now writing an article." Rather, "I'm just roughing this one out." You'll write more freely, and cover lots more territory. Then later, when you think, "I shall now write that article," you will find that a lot of the work has been done. It now may be only a matter of organizing more carefully, and polishing.

3. How long should these articles be?

From 1,500 to 2,500 words. As the preacher said, "Be there. Be brief. Be gone."

4. What about illustrations?

You don't have anything to do with them. If the editor decides that an illustration with your piece would be appropriate, he or she will arrange for it.

5. How should the finished manuscript look?

Professional. Typed, double-spaced, of course. (Editors will not read handwritten manuscripts.) If you are not using an electric typewriter with cartridge ribbons, get a good supply of black typing ribbons for your older model. Don't economize on ribbons. When a ribbon begins to go gray, remove it and save it for the rough composition work of every day.

If you use a word processor, be sure the printer produces a "letter quality" manuscript—preferably not in dot matrix type, which is very hard on the eyes.

Don't economize on paper, either. Leave wide margins, top, bottom and sides. For your own sanity, don't be stingy if you're using carbon paper—it, too, is relatively cheap, and it's maddening to try to read your own dim copy when the original is out.

In typing, be sure your keys are clean; scrub them with alcohol or use commercial cleaner on ink-clogged ones. Resist overstrikes, and don't ever x out. Avoid pencil corrections. An occasional one doesn't hurt, but messy pencil changes break the reading flow and are irritating (and unprofessional). Better to retype.

6. How do I mail it?

Very short pieces, up to 1,000 words, may be folded in thirds and mailed in letter-size white envelopes—with sufficient postage. Longer ones may be folded once in the middle and submitted in 6 × 9″ or 7 × 10″ Manila envelopes; pieces 2,000 to 2,500 words or more should be mailed flat in a large Manila envelope in which you have inserted a lightweight piece of cardboard to protect the manuscript.

Always enclose a stamped, self-addressed envelope, rather than loose postage. Invest in a small postal scale so that you can weigh your manuscripts—and be sure to use enough postage.

7. When do I send it out?

Not until you're sure you've made the manuscript as perfect as possible. It's best to wait a few days after you have finished it, then reread to catch typing errors or little things you may have missed before. Sometimes a few passages have to be rewritten—perhaps only a lead or an ending. Invariably there is something that needs touching up before you mail it.

If the article is seasonal, submit it at least six months before the target date.

8. Do I need to copyright my article?

Under the law, copyright is secured automatically when the work is set down for the first time in written form. In addition, most magazines are copyrighted, and if your work appears in such a publication, it is automatically protected by this blanket copyright notice. Although *technically* you don't need to put a copyright notice (Copyright 1986 John Doe) on the first page of your manuscript, it's probably a good idea to do so as your manuscript makes the rounds of publishers.

9. What about rights?

Most magazines buy first rights only, which means that after your article is published, you are free to sell reprint or "second" rights in that piece to a second magazine. Some publications buy all rights, but they can do so only if you agree to such a sale by signing a written statement.

Marketing

1. Where do I submit?

To the most appropriate magazine — in other words, one that uses this type of article and would be likely to be interested in the subject you have chosen.

Before you write it, you should have one, or several, magazines in mind. If you're just starting out, you should be aware of the fact that although the major national magazines are open to good work from newcomers, the competition is very keen, since your work is being considered along with that of professionals. Don't be intimidated, however. Write your best, then *choose* the best magazines on your list, knowing that if rejected there are plenty of smaller ones to try. These include dozens of regionals, in-flight magazines, publications tied to fraternal organizations, and a crop of less well known women's magazines — so many of which are good markets for articles from the heart. Other good outlets are the religious and inspirational magazines, newspaper supplements and even some trade journals.

2. How do I find out about these magazines and whether they're in the market for articles from the heart?

By studying the writers' magazines and markets, and by studying the magazines themselves. Browse on supermarket newsstands while waiting in line at the checkout counter. Use your time in the doctor's waiting room. Ask friends to save their magazines of special interest. Get religious publications from friends of different denominations; fraternal magazines like *The Elks Magazine* and *The Rotarian*, from members; pick up *Ford Times*, *Volkswagen World*, etc., from dealers. Don't overlook the reading racks in churches, or places of business. The art-of-living booklets there provide another market for your article, either as a reprint or an original.

Study all these publications for total content and tone. Then, when you find a good creative article, analyze *it*, to see what made it acceptable.

I cannot emphasize too strongly the importance of trying these other fields if you really wish to place your work. I have had students who were on the verge of giving up when they discovered them and began to sell.

3. How do you analyze published articles?

Mark and clip. Read with pencil and scissors. In marking, note the lead, and how often it is tied into the final paragraph. I mark *A* for Anecdote in the margin, and frequently count these anecdotes — A.#1, A.#2, A.#3 — etc. *D* is for discussion. *Q* for quotes. If a memory device or symbol is used, I note it. If the style is particularly pleasing, I write an enthusiastic: STYLE! across the top. Apt figures of speech should also be underscored.

The writer who really wants to improve is his own best teacher. And his texts are these published pieces that he wants to emulate.

4. Is a query necessary before submitting articles?

An article from the heart is so subjective that this is a hard question to answer. If the manuscript runs over 1,500 words, yes, I think you should query. Anything under that is really not necessary. On very short articles, 1,000 to 1,500 words, write the entire piece and submit it. Selling these idea pieces depends so much on style and actual treatment, most editors prefer seeing the whole thing.

On the longer ones, 2,000 words or more, a query is in order, as you will be going into the subject more deeply, using more references. It gives the editor a chance to tell you if he already has something of that nature in the works, and can save you effort.

5. How do you prepare a query letter?

State the title and idea immediately, giving a sample treatment of the type you will be using in the opening paragraph. Then briefly summarize the general contents of the proposed article. Give your qualifications for writing it, and the approximate word length. Stop.

If your work has appeared in any of the important magazines, name a few of them. If you've sold primarily to lesser publications it's okay to say, "I've written for a number of magazines." You needn't be specific. If you haven't sold anything as yet, say nothing. Above all, *don't* list a lot of magazines the editor may never have heard of. And *don't* inform him that you are President of a writer's club and this article has just won a prize in your annual contest. (No editor is ever impressed by the acclaim of amateurs.)

6. **To whom should this letter, or the article itself, be addressed?**

To the Managing Editor, by name, as listed on the masthead of the most recent issue of the magazine, or to the Articles Editor, also by name, if listed, or to some appropriate editor. These associate editors receive less mail than their superiors, and are more likely to pay attention to you. Also, it's to their credit when they bring in an acceptable piece of work.

7. **Do I need an agent?**

Reputable agents won't bother with articles by beginners or pieces that don't bring in big payments. When an agent sells an article for you for $500, his commission (10 percent) is only $50. And if you are willing to sell an article to a small magazine for $25, an agent's commission would come to only $2.50, hardly worth his while.

My best advice to beginners is to send these highly subjective ("creative") articles out on their own and hope for the best. If you should make some big sales, agents will be asking you to let them have a chance at selling your work.

How to Get Along With Editors

1. Submit only clean, double-spaced *original* typewritten copy on good white paper. (Never use erasable bond or colored paper or onionskin.) Never submit carbons or photocopies. If you use a word processor, use a printer that produces letter-quality copy—not dot matrix.

2. Submit only one manuscript at a time. (A group of two or three very short sketches would be acceptable, however.) Never deluge an editor with a collection of rejects or even new articles. Let him give his undivided attention (you hope) to one article, before rejecting or accepting it.

3. If querying, submit only one *idea* for a proposed article at a time. "Never give an editor his choice of several," a very fine editor once told me. "In picking one he's automatically turning down the others, remember. Try him on each, one at a time."

4. Send only material that is appropriate to the magazine.

This is mere good marketing sense. An article on weaning a baby could scarcely find a place in *Travel & Leisure*, or the story of how you saved your marriage in *National Geographic*. Yet, some writers bombard the magazines blindly, without bothering to find out what they could conceivably use by reading and studying recent issues. This not only wastes your time and postage, but it irritates the very busy people who have to return all this hopelessly inappropriate material.

I have known many young writers who began to sell regularly, once they made a real study of the markets, particularly the smaller ones, and began to slant their articles to the market needs.

Such writers know their markets, and what is appropriate for them. Editors appreciate writers who show this kind of judgment.

5. A brief letter citing the article by title and identifying yourself is good practice, although I have sold many articles cold, without an accompanying line. If you do write a letter, *don't* do any of the following:

Don't ask the editor what his needs are; you're supposed to know.

Don't ask for a free sample copy at the time you submit your manuscript. Get one first and study it. Better yet, borrow or buy one if it's on the newsstands.

Don't ask for advice or criticism.

Don't say you're just a beginner and will sell cheap, or even let him have the work for nothing. (Nobody should be that desperate.)

Don't put a price on your work. In fact, say nothing about payment. The magazine has its rates, and if your article is accepted, you will be paid accordingly.

Don't tell the editor your life story. Especially your problems — how the house just burned down, your husband has eloped with a belly dancer, leaving you with the sole support of nine children, one of them chronically ill. Editors are not social workers; their job is to find and pay for acceptable material.

6. Don't pester an editor for reports.

Many magazines are infernally slow; this you have to accept. A delay may mean that they are simply swamped and have not had time to consider your contribution. Or it may mean that they are seriously considering it and need more time to make up their minds. The best thing to do is to have so much material in the mail that you don't waste your own time worrying about the fate of a single piece.

However, a courteous prod after six or eight weeks is okay. I have written such letters on a number of occasions. Here's a sample: "According to my records, my article, "_____," was submitted to your magazine on January 21. I wonder if it reached you safely, and if you have come to a decision concerning it." Suffering in silence may be noble, but manuscripts do sometimes get lost in the mail, or land at the bottom of the wrong pile.

7. Don't accuse editors of stealing your ideas.

Editors and publishers are honest, or they couldn't stay in business long. If, after returning an article you submitted, a magazine publishes a piece on a similar topic, they may have had it on hand long before yours showed up. Or they may have received a much better article on the same subject later.

Sometimes a staff writer is assigned to work with or for an amateur whose idea is too good to turn down, but whose presentation is not up to the magazine's standards. In this case, the author who suggested the idea is always consulted and paid.

Writers must operate on faith, as in other areas of life. The last thing they can afford to do is to develop an attitude of skepticism and suspicion toward editors and publishers.

8. Never resubmit a manuscript that an editor has previously rejected—unless you call his attention to that fact, and have some very good reason, such as a revision, to ask him to reconsider. If you have exhausted all your markets and feel that you must start over, rewrite the article and tell the editor why you think it's now more appropriate to his needs. (The magazine itself may have undergone a change of policy.) Otherwise forget it until the editor leaves and another is in charge.

9. Be friendly but businesslike. This is just as important after you've sold an editor as it is before. In the first blush of acceptance, you may love him madly and imagine the feeling is mutual. Just remember he or she is dealing with a lot of other authors, too.

It is sometimes desirable to get to the cities where the magazines to which you've submitted material are published and meet editors in person. But *not* until you have sold some material to them and have other articles to discuss. Editors just don't have the time or energy to interview hopefuls, however promising. "Sell me something, then come see me," is the attitude they almost have to take. Once this happy circumstance occurs, you may discover that you have interests in common, and in time a genuine friendship may develop. This bond between editor and author is one of the rewards of the writing profession.

But in the beginning at least, it is always firmly rooted on one thing: Your product geared to his needs. A friendly professionalism.

CHAPTER EIGHTEEN

Making the Most of Your Talent

Talent is a gift. You had nothing to do with receiving yours, nor I with receiving mine. But I am convinced that each of us is given his talent for a reason. And that having talent, any talent, but particularly one for writing, imposes two responsibilities: to use it, and to use it for good. "There is a *duty*," that wise teacher also said.

Surely that first duty is: *Talent must not go to waste.*

What is the true cause of wasted talent? I think it's primarily a lack of that sense of responsibility or duty. Too often talent is regarded as a mere adornment, something with which to amuse yourself and dazzle your friends. That's how it seems when one is very young. I used to write long continued stories which the kids passed around in school (ending when the tablet paper ran out). I dashed off poems dedicated to everybody in sight and read aloud on all possible occasions. I even wrote my own declamatory pieces. And it was all part of a heady show-off syndrome.

Yet deep beneath all this ran a fierce compulsion. I *had* to write. Even minus an audience, into a vast notebook, late at night, I had to write. And what clinched this compulsion for me and turned it into a *profession* were the words, "There is a duty."

People who fail to follow up their own bright promise seem to lack this compulsion. It is much easier, of course, to regard your talent not simply as essential if awesome equipment for an important calling, but as an ornament to be kept in a drawer. You know it's there, your pretty little talent, and you can always dust it off and don it if you wish — when you're "inspired." Or delight admiring friends by doing witty newsletters for some organization or by composing the club show.

Yet you know, deep in your guts you know, you can and should be doing so much more.

The list of excuses for wasted talent is endless. But those who take their talent as a serious responsibility appraise this obstacle course and figure out their priorities: "Is it more important to attend that meeting or to get on with my article? . . . I have a doctor's appointment at three, but if I get started at nine, that still gives me five hours at the typewriter. No, subtract an hour for interruptions, and that still leaves four for writing."

When people ask how I've done it — raised four children while writing hundreds of magazine pieces and thirty books — I tell them: "I'm disciplined and I'm organized." I learned early to forgo temptations and to budget time. Any household has a reasonable facsimile of a schedule. I planned my writing hours to fit into it. When I lost a day to the emergencies that befall any family, I made it up on weekends.

The writer's *second* responsibility: *Use your talent for good*. Not to preach or exhort or reform necessarily, but to affirm life rather than debase it, to inspire and help and encourage. . . . *"You can write beautiful things for people who crave beautiful things. . . ."* Despite the cynicism, materialism, violence and sex that seem to pervade almost every medium of communication, including the articles in many of today's magazines — despite the avalanche of products that pander to a lust for the perverse, the ugly, the decadent, there is still a vast hunger for things of the spirit, beautiful things. And the writer who is able to nourish and fill that hunger creatively and honestly is beginning to reap incredible and long overdue riches.

I am not talking about pieties and preachments, or writing that simply shuts its eyes and pretends there is no evil or sorrow in the world. But rather writing that shows the basic goodness and decency of human beings despite their trials; that celebrates compassion and love and wonder and all the other things that make life worthwhile.

How to Become a Professional

To make the most of your talent, writing can't be your hobby. It must become your profession. Only then can you reach the most people — those who need and will enjoy what you have to say. But how does the writer of articles or anything else, get to be a pro?

It seems to me that the amateur becomes a professional when he stops *thinking* of himself as an amateur, and regards himself as a serious, dedicated worker in a highly competitive profession. Otherwise he will never develop the professional working habits he must have to succeed.

This means undergoing some severe emotional spasms that may not seem professional in themselves: the longing to write at inconvenient times; the maddening interruptions when you start; the agonizing battle against procrastination; the shock of having your best pieces sometimes go begging; the hours of self-doubt and despair. Or the contrasting ecstasy when you succeed, and it seems for a little while at least that all doors will be open to you for evermore. Also, there are times when you are feted, applauded, made to feel a real celebrity (while a little voice inside you scoffs, knowing the real you so wretchedly well); times when total strangers make a fuss over you—while some of your best friends (you thought) pointedly ignore the fact that you have done anything remotely worthy of notice.

These things constitute just some of the blood, sweat and rejection slips that a real writer must experience on the road to becoming a professional—and thereafter—because, though they let up after a while, or possibly because you are inured to them, for very few people indeed does there ever arrive a halcyon time when all obstacles and difficulties actually stop.

Writers who refuse to stay amateurs develop moral muscles—sheer determination, guts. They go on working in the face of repeated failures. Above all, they develop the kind of self-discipline that says "No!" to the thousands of temptations that would lure them away from their typewriters. This discipline must be continuously practiced—and mastered—if a writer is to develop good professional working habits and become, in the genuine sense of the word, "professional."

Procrastination

Procrastination is the beginning writer's—or amateur's—enemy; habit is his ally, because, once you have become the incurable professional, habit will keep you from procrastinating. "We write," as Thomas Wolfe said, "because we want to write so damn bad." By then we not only want so intensely to write, we *are* writing so constantly that habit drives us to the daily rendezvous, almost against our will at times.

Procrastination takes many forms. The excuses it makes for you are numerous and varied. Major among them are your responsibilities to other people. If you have a job and can't work full-time at your writing, it is doubtful indeed if you can support a family by your typewriter alone. When you get home from working all day (especially if you have a writing job that drains your creative energies), it's not only hard to try to write creatively, but you feel it's not fair to shut yourself away from the family. I couldn't be more sympathetic. It seems to me that anyone who puts in a full day working at something other than his own writing has a double handicap, yet determined men and women do it all the time.

Most families are surprisingly cooperative, once they realize the aspiring authors are in earnest.

Women with young children have a blue-ribbon alibi for postponing their writing. The world is teeming with frustrated, nonwriting mothers who complain that they just *can't* write with all the duties, problems, demands."Wait," you say, until the last child is in school, out of junior high, high school, college, married. But by then, the grandchildren are being left with you just when you're ready to get started on your writing career. By that time anyway, the neglected flower of talent has drooped, wilted and may never be revived. Worse, the habit of putting it off until the *right time comes* may be too deeply ingrained for you to be able to change and buckle down to work at your typewriter.

Sooner or later writers or would-be writers must face the fact that the world will simply not ever stop to let us write.

Even childless people often develop a gift for procrastination that sometimes surpasses that of people with families. They take courses, hold offices in writing clubs, spend hours in libraries doing research, develop impressive filing systems, seek out the company of other writers to discuss ideas, take trips to gather material — do everything but write! *Whereas*, if you have several offspring yelling for attention, such free time as you can wrest from the day is simply too precious to squander. You race to your appointed place at the appointed (or unexpected) hour, and write!

Here are several suggestions:

1. Steer clear of organizations. Let the PTA, political organizations, women's clubs, and company get-togethers struggle along without you. Join even one, and before you know it, you're on a committee or managing a fund-raiser. The writer's job is to write!

This must be modified slightly for parents. If you have school-age children, it isn't possible or fair to ignore the Scout meetings, school concerts, plays, soccer matches, or other activities that are related to their normal growing up. Busy writer-parents can and do and must make room for such; but keep your participation at the minimum level that will square with your own conscience and your youngsters' happiness. (But guard that you're not using conscience as an excuse for procrastination.)

After you do become a professional, with the procrastination problem overcome, there are professional organizations that can be a definite help to you. By then your children will be older, and you won't need to feel guilty at forgoing some of their activities. You may even allow yourself a day off occasionally just for fun. But in the beginning, don't yield to temptation. Stay home and write!

2. Have your own definite place to work. An office, a study, even a screened-off corner of the bedroom. But somewhere strictly your own where you can go — preferably with a door to shut.

Have a big roomy desk there, and the best equipment you can manage. A good typewriter and the kind of chair you find most comfortable. Writing is hard, physical work, so be sure to give yourself whatever comfort you can during the process. At one point when I was having backaches and bouts with bursitis, I invested in a posture chair and the first electric typewriter on the market. The relief was little short of miraculous. Later on, I bought an IBM Selectric typewriter, which uses disposable tapes instead of the old-fashioned ribbons, and has an erasing key. These are wonderful features I could no longer do without. Finally, I succumbed to a word processor and spent an agonized year in a love-hate relationship with it. Love ultimately triumphed. But creative habits are hard to break. I still write my first drafts on my regular typewriter and use the word processor mainly to revise and for final copy. It works like magic for editing and revisions and produces beautiful manuscripts.

Get a filing cabinet so you won't have to waste time trying to find things. On a long trip, take a portable typewriter or a laptop computer along to record ideas. I have found that handwritten notes have a way of being mislaid or not getting transcribed. But if you don't do this, be sure to take clear and detailed notes. Transcribe them as soon as you get home, and file them under whatever headings you have devised, so it will be easy for you to find them later.

Your equipment need not be brand new. You can often pick up cabinets, a desk, even a good used typewriter, at a garage sale or a secondhand store. However you do it, equip yourself professionally, if you want to write professionally.

3. Have a schedule. Write daily at regular hours — early in the morning, or after dinner, if you are employed. Or, if not, during the day between the more predictable activities of the household. Even if your schedule has to be juggled, changed, reshaped as the demands on you alter, the mere fact of *having* a schedule and striving continually to keep it strengthens that invaluable ally — habit.

4. If you are a writer with young children and don't have a job outside your home, get some household help for a few hours a day if you can possibly manage to do so. Even a few hours a week, set aside just for your writing, will make a difference in establishing good writing habits and will help you produce more than you think — if you do it regularly.

5. Be patient with interruptions. Do whatever you can to keep them at a minimum, but stop fighting back when they occur. It only wastes valuable emotional energy and time. Spare yourself and everybody else by maintaining an attitude of stoic but cheerful acceptance. Then get back to work and do the best you can.

6. Write every day, whether or not you have an idea, or are "inspired." The sheer act of putting something down on paper will start generating ideas. And quite often the true inspiration occurs during the act of creating, when you are caught up in the process and become excited by what evolves.

Remember this: Habit, the simple act of going to the same place at the same time whenever humanly possible, and doing the same thing there, can save you from procrastination. After a while you will go for no better reason than that you cannot stay away; the strong but subtle hands of habit will draw you there.

Procrastination is the writer's enemy. Habit is his ally.

Writers Clubs, Conferences and Critics

Writing is said to be a lonely business. But so is almost any art—and a good thing too. Discussing this, an artist-friend once remarked, "Loneliness is the real beginning of living, the beginning of growth. No artist can ever accomplish anything until he can find out who he really is by working alone." This is especially true of writing. Writers must discover their true capacities by wrestling alone with their thoughts.

For me this is not loneliness in the self-sacrificing or depressing sense. My hours at the typewriter are spent in the company of so many intriguing ideas and characters, while normal loneliness is usually suffered in the midst of mere mortals who don't share the emotional highs and lows of writers, or who seem dull by comparison. Yet, writers, like most people, love to talk shop, especially with other writers who speak their language. Thus—writers clubs. And a big, bold sign: **Beware!**

Far too many writers clubs are aggregations of people who like to look, act and talk like writers—but aren't. Either they don't write enough to qualify, or they don't write well enough to sell. And in spending very much time in their company you are psychologically classifying yourself an amateur, and holding back your own advancement as a professional. These clubs may give you emotional support, but even when they elect you to office, award you prizes for your work, and publish it in their journals, they are offering a *substitute* for the recognition and payment you should be receiving on the professional playing field.

Another danger of writers clubs is the criticism generally offered there. The wrong advice from the wrong people can dampen your enthusiasm and confuse you, sometimes with devastating effects. Or it can feed your ego out of all proportion to the actual merit of what you have written. In general, it is a mistake to expose your manuscripts to *anybody* who is not a bona fide professional. This includes wives, husbands, best friends, loving aunts, as well as fellow hopefuls. There are, of course, exceptions: a perceptive teacher who is tuned into the current literary marketplace, an unusually intelligent spouse, a writers group that includes some experienced or knowledgeable people.

How, then, can the beginner learn? He can learn by trial and error, the toughest and in some ways the best teacher. He can also combine and generally cut short some of the trial and error by taking a good writers course conducted by those who know from experience what they're talking about; who can recognize the good things about your work, and point out the things that you ought to consider changing, with suggestions for how you might do so. But let me state firmly here that *no writers course ever taught anyone how to write. Writers courses can only take people with talent, who already know how to write and teach them how to write better.* And, with hard work, more successfully.

Writing courses need not be expensive. Some excellent ones are given in adult education programs of high schools and colleges, the YMCA and YWCA, community adult education centers, lifelong learning programs in many major universities and colleges, and other senior citizens groups.

There are also correspondence courses, but they seem to me to have a built-in drawback: you may not finish them or get your money's worth. Many good ones are offered by colleges, and some writers prefer correspondence courses because of the definite assignments and written criticisms. But if you have to depend upon assignments or goads of this kind to make you write, you may lack the basic qualifications that are absolutely essential if you are ever to become a professional writer: talent plus drive.

Don't keep taking courses. If one, or at the most two, haven't really helped you, forget it.

A good writers conference can be immensely stimulating. When the workshops, classes and panels are conducted by experienced professionals who are also able to convey know-how and enthusiasm, the time and money couldn't be better spent. But again, don't be a perennial conference-goer. Dive into one or two and soak up all you can. Then go home and *swim*, until you become so proficient on your own that one day they'll be asking you back to teach the next class!

The crux of the whole learning process, however, is you, the writer: your talent; your determination to learn, as you can learn by reading, studying, observing, *writing*; your willingness to so arrange your life, at whatever cost, that writing *does* become your real profession. A glorious, exacting, enslaving, freeing, life-enhancing profession at which you work every day, in artistic, emotional, but always professional terms.

The article from the heart is but *one* form of literary endeavor, and a good one both for the writers and their readers.

If you can write good articles from the heart, you may also be able to write other things—short stories, books—works upon which your true achievements as a writer will rest, you hope.

One important bonus from writing such articles is that they are such a natural springboard for books. I know many writers whose books evolved either as a collection or an expansion of their articles. My own case is not unique. As I said earlier, it was a long apprenticeship in the magazines that led directly to my column, "Love and Laughter," in the Washington, D.C., *Star*. Which, in turn, led directly to the publication of so many books.

At this writing, the hardcover trade sales of my books are at least six million copies. These, plus book clubs, foreign editions and paperbacks, make the total count astronomical. And all because the things I longed to express came not from outside sources, but from my own observations, experiences, reflections and feelings. In short, from the heart. The key was simply to express those ideas and emotions in a way that makes them applicable to others.

Meanwhile, books or not, the author of warm, sincere articles from the heart receives the greatest stimulus anyone can have to keep at it: publication in reputable magazines that pay you for your work. Payments may be small and far apart at first; but whatever their size or frequency, they are vital signal fires to light the way and help reaffirm your faith in yourself.

At the same time, you are also realizing rewards that are equally significant: a chance to share your own story, what you have experienced, what you have learned; moments of beauty and love and inspiration too compelling to keep. And with all this, the knowledge that somewhere out in a chaotic and troubled world somebody is laughing because of you, somebody is kinder, more compassionate, more understanding, more sure of his own dreams or his own strength to carry on.

In writing articles from the heart you are not only lighting your own often dark paths as a writer, you are lighting the way for other people, too.

Index

A

ABC of Style — A Guide to Plain English, The, 135
Advice article, 8, 57-61, 90, 91, 110, 125-126
  defined, 9
  organizational pattern for, 104
Agent, 151
Alliteration, 117, 142-143
American Home, 32
Anecdotes, 83, 87-90, 102-104, 106
  about children, 39-44
Angle of interpretation, 84, 97
  See also Tone
Aristotle on style, 132
Articles from the heart, 7-11
  audience for, 83
  length of, 147
  principles of, 70
  rewards of writing, 163-164
  selling, 7
  as springboard for books, 163
  ways to improve, 110-120
  See also Creative article
As Tall as My Heart, 79
"As told to" article, 25
At Christmas the Heart Goes Home, 79, 142-143
Attitude toward material, 92, 94-96
Audience for articles from the heart, 83

B

Beauty in Your Own Backyard, 79
Better Homes and Gardens, 10, 20-21, 33-36, 105, 119-120, 126, 142

Books
  article writing as springboard for, 163
  of column collections, 78-80
  of nostalgia, 49-50
  sales of, by author, 163
Booklets, art-of-living, 149
Bowen, Elizabeth, rhythm example by, 144

C

Characterization, 89, 112-113
Children, articles about, 37-44, 111
Clichés, 136-137
Color, 110, 111-112
Columns, 73-80
Comparisons
  See Contrast and comparison
Conclusions, 83, 90
Contrast and comparison, 107, 110-111, 114
Controversial topics, 51-56
  See also Protest and controversy
Conversation(s), 18-19, 103
Copyright, 148
Correspondence courses, 162
Creative article(s), 7-11, 31, 92, 150
  categories of, 8-11
  five fundamentals of, 83-90
  form of, 102-104
  length of, 147
  See also individual categories
Creative writer, 24, 66, 126
Criticism, 152, 161-162

D

Deal, Dewey, 1-2, 73
Death as subject, 93
Dialogue, 89-90, 103, 104, 118-119
Dixon, George, on humor, 70

E

Editors, getting along with, 151-154
Elks Magazine, 30
Equipment for writing, 159-160
Essays and sketches, 8, 10, 71-73, 104

F

Family Circle, 58-59, 107-109
Figures of speech, 138-139
First-person stories, 24
Flashback, 25, 26-27
Flesch, Rudolf, on writing style, 135
Focus, 31, 32, 47-48, 97-100
Form, 103-104
    See also Organization
Formulas, writing, 102
Foster, Constance, rhythm example by, 144

G

Generalizations and specifics, 115-116
Good Reading Rack, 59
Guideposts, 9, 26, 39-42

H

Hammerstein, Oscar, quote from, 127
Hold Me Up a Little Longer, Lord, 79
House Beautiful, 32
Humor, 8, 10-11, 67, 91, 95
    inappropriate, 64, 86
    logic in, 65-66
    timing in writing, 64-65
Humorous articles, 62-70, 91, 95, 104, 113

I

Idea(s), article, 83-85, 87
    getting, 12-23, 103
    querying magazines on, 151
    sources of, 16-22, 61, 118
    stealing of, by editors, 153
Illustrations, 147
Imagery, 138-139
Inspirational article, 8, 11, 87, 91
I've Got to Talk to Somebody, God, 78-79

J

Jargon, 135-136
Johnson, Samuel, on writing, 2

L

Ladies' Home Journal, 106
L'Engle, Madeleine, on writing, 102
Lord, Let Me Love, 79
"Love and Laughter" newspaper column, 67-68, 78, 79, 163

M

Magazine(s)
    rates, 152
    religious, 38
    small, as beginner markets, 33, 38
Mailing manuscripts, 148
Man, The, 32
Manuscript(s)
    mailing, 148
    preparing, 147-148, 151
    submitting, 150-154
Marketing methods, 149-154
Market(s)
    beginning, small publications as, 33, 38
Marquand, John, description of, as color example, 111-112
Marriage articles, 31-37, 58-59, 111
Maugham, Somerset, on style, 135
McCall's, 37, 72

Memoirs, 45-50
  See also Nostalgia
Memory devices, 116-120
Messiah, The, 79
Metaphors, 137
  See also Figures of speech

N

Name-dropping, 128
Names, real, in anecdotes, 88-89
Nation's Business, 59-61
Newspaper column, 73-80
  book collections of, 78-80
Nobody Else Will Listen, 79
Nostalgia, articles of, 8, 10, 45-50,
  86, 111, 112
Nostalgic books, 49-50
Notebook
  for anecdotes, 39
  for ideas, 22-23, 73

O

Opening of article, 104-106, 120
Organization, 102-109
Originality in style, 136-137, 144-145
Outline, 146-147

P

Pace, 100-101
Parents and children, articles about,
  37-44, 111
Pedantry, 136
Permission for quotes, 129-131
Personal experience, articles of, 8,
  24-30, 87, 111
  defined, 9
  flashback, use of, in, 25, 26-27
  organizational pattern for, 104
  tone in, 91-92
  See also Marriage; Nostalgia;
    Parents and children
Physical afflictions as subject, 93-94
Poems, permission to quote, 130

Point of view, 92, 96
Premise, basic, 92
Procrastination, 157-161
Professional writer, 156-157
Protest and controversy, articles of, 8,
  9-10, 86, 91, 110-111
  organizational pattern for, 104,
    106-109
  quotes in, 125-126
  topics for, 51-56
PTA Magazine, The, 96

Q

Query letter, 54, 150, 151
  for newspaper column, 73-74
Quotes, 125-131
  obtaining, 128-129
  permission to use, 129-131
  sources of, 127, 129

R

Reader identification, 29-30, 49, 70,
  83
Reader's Digest, 9, 10, 21, 34, 35, 96,
  119-120
Redundancy, 141-142
Religious magazines, 38
Reminiscence, article of, 104
  See also Nostalgia
Rhythm and style, 132, 134, 143-144
Rights, 148-149

S

Saturday Review, 111-112
Seasonal articles, submitting, 148
Self-help articles, 57-61
Self-satire articles, 67-68
Sentences, length of, 143
Sex as subject, 94
Shalit, Gene, interview by, 83
Similes, 137
  See also Figures of speech
Sketches, 8, 10, 71-73, 87

Songs, permission to quote, 130
Specifics, 114-116
Structure, 83, 86-87
   See also Organization
Style, 31, 83, 85-86, 100, 113-114
   developing, 132-135
   improving, 135-145
   See also Tone
Subject, wrong, 92-94
   See also Theme
Summary, article, 83, 90
Symbols, 117-118

T

Talent for writing, 155-164
Theme, 103-104
"Think" pieces, 7
Three from Galilee, 79
Time for Faith, A Time for Love, A, 79
Time to write, best, 147
Timeliness, 110, 113-114
Titles, 31, 57, 63
   finding, 121-122
   kinds of, 123-125
To Help You Through the Hurting, 79
To Treasure Our Days, 79
"Today Show" interview, 83
Today's Health, 10, 54-55
Tone, 43, 86, 91-101, 110, 111
   See also Style
Tull, Jewell Bothwell, 2
Tull, Toppy, 2
Two from Galilee, 79

V

Viewpoint, personal, in marriage
   articles, 36
Vocabulary and timeliness, 113-114

W

Washington, D.C. Star, newspaper
   column, 67-68, 74-75, 79, 163
Wolfe, Thomas, on writing, 157
Woolf, Virginia, on essays, 72-73
Woman, The, 32-33
Woman's Conversations with God, A, 79
Woman's Day, 79
Word(s),
   repetition of, 140-141
   right, 139-140
Writers clubs, 161-162
Writers conferences, 162
Writing
   discipline and, 156
   equipment, 159-160
   habit, 160-161
   methods, 146-149
   organization and, 156
   and procrastination, 157-161
   responsibilities in, 155-156
   schedule, 160
   talent, 155-156
   time, best, for, 147
Writing courses, 162
Writing profession, 155, 156-157

Y

You and I and Yesterday, 10, 49, 79
Young Man from Nazareth, The, 79
Your Life, 32